Massacre of Glencoe

John Buchan

Lang**Syne**

PUBLISHING

WRITING *to* REMEMBER

Note

In this essay in reconstruction I have tried to include no detail which has not a warrant from contemporary evidence, or is not a legitimate deduction from such evidence. The only liberty I have taken is now and then to state boldly as fact what should strictly be qualified by a 'probably'.

John Buchan

Reprinted 1992, 1995, 2002, 2003, 2005, 2007, 2009, 2010, 2011, 2012, 2015, 2016 and 2018.

Lang**Syne**

PUBLISHING

WRITING *to* REMEMBER

79 Main Street, Newtongrange,
Midlothian EH22 4NA
Tel: 0131 344 0414 Fax: 0845 075 6085
E-mail: info@lang-syne.co.uk
www.langsyneshop.co.uk

Printed by Printwell Ltd
© Lang Syne Publishers Ltd 2018

ISBN 978-1-85217-164-3

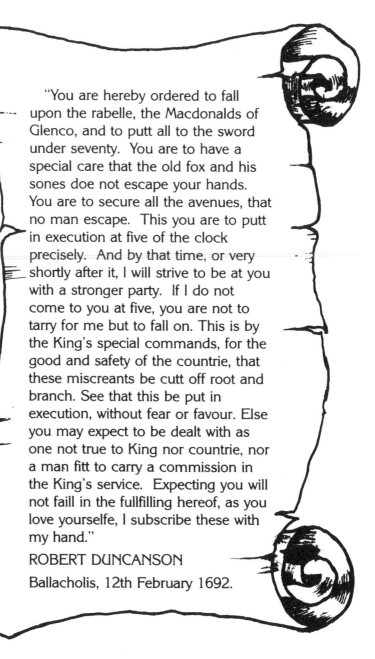

"You are hereby ordered to fall upon the rabelle, the Macdonalds of Glenco, and to putt all to the sword under seventy. You are to have a special care that the old fox and his sones doe not escape your hands. You are to secure all the avenues, that no man escape. This you are to putt in execution at five of the clock precisely. And by that time, or very shortly after it, I will strive to be at you with a stronger party. If I do not come to you at five, you are not to tarry for me but to fall on. This is by the King's special commands, for the good and safety of the countrie, that these miscreants be cutt off root and branch. See that this be put in execution, without fear or favour. Else you may expect to be dealt with as one not true to King nor countrie, nor a man fitt to carry a commission in the King's service. Expecting you will not faill in the fullfilling hereof, as you love yourselfe, I subscribe these with my hand."

ROBERT DUNCANSON

Ballacholis, 12th February 1692.

Letter that ordered the Massacre of Glencoe

INTRODUCTION

The Massacre of Glencoe was one of the most shameful and disgraceful acts of betrayal in Scotland's long and turbulent history.

On the orders of the king, soldiers who had enjoyed the hospitality of the MacDonald clan for 11 days, rose in the night and butchered their hosts.

Maclan, the chief, 33 men, two women and two children were either put to the sword or shot dead. Many others perished in snow blizzards as they tried to escape.

Not content with murdering the MacDonalds the soldiers even burned their homes to the ground and destroyed their livestock.

In these pages master storyteller John Buchan tells how an innocent mistake by Maclan ended in slaughter. Many Scottish clans had remained loyal to King James II after he was replaced on the throne by William in 1689 and in an effort to unite the nation the Government announced a truce in August, 1691.

All clan chiefs who swore an oath of allegiance before January 1, 1692, would be regarded as loyal subjects and no action would be taken against them.

But Maclan left his decision to sign until the last moment and then found, due to administration problems, that he was unable to take the oath until January 6.

Meantime, men in high Government office had decided to make an example of the little clan in Glencoe while sparing others who still had not signed.

On February 13, 1692, five weeks after their chief swore loyalty to King William, a force of 920 regular soldiers was unleashed against 200 MacDonalds .... in the words of the song, like murdering foxes among helpless sheep, they murdered the house of MacDonald.

CHAPTER ONE
The Fort of Inverlochy

The Governor's room in the fort was a cheerless place on that afternoon of late December. It was barely furnished; a couple of travelling-chests, a big deal table crowded with papers, one or two chairs of local make with seats of untanned hide, and a camp bed in a corner. On the floor were skins of deer, and on one wall a stand of arms. The peat fire was burning badly, as it always did in a north-west wind, and the blue smoke from it clouded without warming the air. The small windows were plastered with drifting snow. The man who sat writing at the table stopped to listen to the gale, which howled outside and deadened the tramp of the sentry's feet. He shivered, and turned up the collar of his military greatcoat.

Colonel John Hill was an old man, well on in his sixties, with a lean tired face and washed-out eyes. He held himself erect, but rheumatism crippled his movements. That spring he had been sick for three months with fever and, though his health had improved in the summer, the wet autumn had brought a relapse and he had felt strangely inert and vigourless. Moreover, at no time in his long career had he been so cumbered with perplexities. He had got little out of life, and now the burden of it was becoming too heavy for him. Long ago he had lost all ambition and asked only for peace and a modest comfort, but these blessings were still denied him.

He took from a file a copy of the letter he had written to Lord Tarbat eight months before — Tarbat had always been his friend. "I find illwishers grow upon me," he read, "and some great men. They say I am old, and would, I think, have me to reduce all the Highlands myself, which, if I could do, there would be as little need for them as there is for this garrison. I would his Majesty would give me any other place where I could be serviceable to him, and let some emulators take this, and then I might be quiet." That plaint reminded him of the Psalms of David and he muttered a verse or two to himself. He had always been a religious man.

The weather matched his mood. He let his pen drop, sank his chin into his greatcoat, and permitted his mind to run over his past vicissitudes and present distractions. For forty years and more he had been a soldier. Long ago in Cromwell's day he had served under George Monk in Fitch's regiment, and had come from Ruthven to command in this very fort of Inverlochy which Monk had built to bridle the wild Highlandmen. He had been young then and had loved the service, and the great Duke of Albemarle was a leader he had been proud to follow. He himself had been popular with the natives, and had hunted and fished with the chiefs; many a gift of salmon and venison had reached him from the hills; he had proclaimed Richard Cromwell in the market-place in the presence of Lochiel and Glengarry, and when King Charles came back to his own he had surrendered Inverlochy to Lochiel in all friendliness. He was a soldier, and knew no politics.

Since then he had heard the drum in various quarters of the world, but he had always cherished happy memories of Scotland. He had corresponded with the old laird of Culloden and with his son Duncan, the present laird, and he had now Duncan's brother John as his major. When the Revolution came he had been Constable of Belfast Castle and had made a stout stand against the Irish rebels; but for him, he believed the victory of the Boyne would not have been achieved. His reward had been to be sent to Scotland in June 1690, to take over the Inverlochy garrison which General Hugh Mackay had revived on Monk's plan.

There had been trouble from the first. Mackay, whose temper had not been improved by Killiecrankie, was captious, vain and irritable, with none of Monk's calm supremacy. The Jacobite commander-in-chief, Thomas Buchan, had indeed been soundly beaten by Sir Thomas Livingstone at Cromdale, and had since been vainly attempting what Mackay called the 'chicane' of war in Aberdeenshire, but it had been feared that any day he might come west to trouble Lochaber. Hill had felt himself called to too arduous a service. Scotland was a bleak place for a man who was in failing health and growing old. He considered that he deserved more comfortable rewards. The knighthood which was his due still tarried. He wanted a pension. He wanted a good regiment, and had only got an amalgam of the weak remnants of Kenmure's and Glencairn's. Above all he wanted to be paid monies due to him. All his life he had been spending out of his own pocket on the public service; on providing a minister's stipend in the days of Cromwell; on garrisoning Belfast; and now on finding Inverlochy in the bare necessaries of life and defence.

His one pride was this fort of his, for of the policy which it exemplified he had been the chief begetter, and it carried the memories of his far-away youth. It had been christened, Fort William, and the new works had been erected in eleven days. Mackay had found fault with the old site in the angle of the River Nevis, on the plea that it could be commanded from higher ground — as if the clans had much artillery! But he had made a solid business of the defence — fosse, wall twenty feet high palisaded around, *glacis* and *chemin couvert*. The chief trouble had been the barracks inside for the garrison of more than a thousand men, for no wood could be got in that countryside of scrub birch and hazel, and the Government were slow in sending timber from Leith and the Clyde. Every week he had to write to Melville or Tarbat or Livingstone pleading for supplies.

It was not Mackay's blame. Before he left the Scottish command he had written to the Duke of Hamilton — Hill had seen the letter — declaring that the Inverlochy fort was "the most important of the kingdom at present," and urging that "it be by no means neglected." But supplies still came laggardly. The garrison was short of ammunition, ill-clad and ill-shod; it was provisioned from Argyll and Kintyre, but food was constantly running low, and the men's rations were often only meal and water and a tot of *Aqua vitae*. Small wonder that their temper was getting ugly.

There had been other troubles, some of them happily past. The first garrison had been four companies of the Angus regiment, four of Argyll's, and nine of the laird of Grant's. The Angus men, and especially their chaplain, did not like the place, and they had been sent to Flanders; Hill had regretted it, for they were good soldiers. After that he had been left with Grant's and Argyll's, and now they were all Argyll's. These last were Highlanders, and he was a little doubtful whether hawks could be trusted to pick out hawks' eyes. Angus's whiggamores were a troublesome folk, but more dependable. Then there was the question of a deputy-governor and lieutenant-colonel for the garrison. He refused to have a Highlander, and in the end got a certain James Hamilton, a Lowlander with good connections — a competent man, but a difficult subordinate, for he was in private correspondence with Sir John Dalrymple, the Secretary of State for Scotland, and Livingstone, who had succeeded Mackay as commander-in-chief, wrote to him more often than to the Governor.

Lastly, there was the eternal anxiety about communications. There were three routes to Inverlochy: one by sea from the south, and two by land. Of the land routes, that from Inverness had to pass through Glengarry's country, and that from Atholl through Badenoch was commanded by Keppoch, and in any case was not open till the middle of June. The only safe communication was by water. But the Government showed no sense of the importance of the sea route, they sent too few frigates and kept up no regular system of supply. Yet Lochaber was a powder magazine, a turn of fortune's wheel on the Continent and French ships of war would be off its coast, Buchan and the other Jacobite leaders were still at large. Hill never sent his patrols into Brae Lochaber without a fear lest they should bring back news that the fiery cross had gone round and that the heather was ablaze.

He disliked politics, but he had perforce to take a hand in them, and a fine confusion they presented to a simple fighting man. At the head of all was William, a great king and a fine soldier whom Hill revered; but how could one who had just finished a stiff campaign in Ireland, and was now engaged in a life-and-death struggle in Flanders, spare time for the affairs of this distant northern land? Yet William had recognised the merits of the Inverlochy scheme; a namesake of Hill's own, a captain of Leven's, had seen him at Chester on the matter nineteen months ago, and the King had peremptorily ordered the Council to supply anything needed for the work. That was well enough, but the King's viceregents in Scotland had no such clearness of purpose. To a plain soldier like himself they seemed to be concerned more about their personal aggrand-isement than about the peace of the realm, and to rate the settlement of their Kirk higher than the pacification of Scotland. He was a devout man, but he had no patience with their religious bickerings. The fortunes of the land were on a razor's edge, and those lawyer folk would not see it. They squabbled about their family interests, when a single reverse to British arms on the Continent might stir the Highlands and send down on the Lowlands a spate of desperate men.

There was Melville, with his big head and ashen face and mean presence, who thought more of advancing his son Leven's career than of soldierly measures of defence. A Presbyterian of the old rock and no doubt an honest man, but a slow and tortuous one. There was Tarbat, handsome and genial, but slippery like all of the Mackenzie blood. And now there was the Master of Stair, another lawyer, who was said to hold the chief place in the King's confidence. Hill had never met him, but he had heard much about the Dalrymples. His mother was said to have been a witch, and the old Viscount, his father, was reputed the craftiest brain in the kingdom. Sir John, now Master of Stair, was one of the new Secretaries of State; he was hated by the Presbyterians for having been King's advocate under James, and by the Jacobites for having shamelessly turned his coat. No man had ever in his hearing said a good word for Sir John, but all had spoken with solemnity of his devilish subtlety and cold relentlessness of purpose. But even if these civilians meant honestly, they were hampered by utter ignorance of the Highlander. Tarbat was different; he knew his own race, and Hill had found him the easiest to work with. The others were Lowlanders, knowing less of the Gael than Hill knew of the Kamchatkans, but with an ancestral hatred and distrust of all who wore tartan. There were indeed two Highlanders who had the knowledge, but they were scarcely men to ride the ford with. There was Argyll, who had offered to serve against his own father and for whom none had a kind word. And there was Breadalbane.

The last was the personage who for the past twelve months had been giving Hill his most anxious thoughts. He had known him of old, and trusted him not at all. No one living had had a stranger career, for this Highland chief had made himself great and rich by a combination of the methods of attorney and cateran. As Sir John Campbell of Glenorchy he had lent money to the bankrupt Earl of Caithness, and foreclosed on his title and estates; he had fought a battle at Wick to establish his

*Breadalbane had made himself rich and powerful
through devious means.*

claim; being deprived of the title he had won as mortgagee, he
had got a new patent as Earl of Breadalbane; he had extended
his territory from Loch Awe to Loch Tay by beggaring his
neighbours; he had been deep in every Jacobite plot, and yet he
had some inexplicable secret influence at William's court. Next
to Argyll he was the most powerful man in the Highlands, but he
was less disliked than Argyll, for he had a certain surface
geniality. His avarice was notorious, but he could be friendly
when it cost him nothing. Mackay had hated him, and Mackay
for all his megrims was an acute judge of character.

Breadalbane had no love for Inverlochy, for he had a scheme of his own — that the Government should make it worth the while of the chiefs to submit and live at peace. This was a popular policy among the Scottish statesmen of Highland blood, for each wanted to be chosen as intermediary, since doubtless there would be pickings in the business. There was sense in the proposal, Hill thought, if it were adopted side by side with his own and Mackay's scheme of forts and garrisons. Some of the money allotted might be used to buy up the disputed feudal superiorities which were a sore point with the clans; Argyll, for example, had certain claims to superiority over Macdonald lands, and there could be no peace till that thorn was plucked out. Hill himself had been inclined to make the attempt when he first came to Scotland, the efforts of Campbell of Cawdor having failed, and he had spent some weary weeks travelling the Highlands without success. The sum named was too small, only £2000, and the proffered peerages found no acceptors. Hill's reason assented to the plan, but his instincts were against it, and he feared its maleficent extension. The time had not yet come to trust the Highlanders; a just and firm policy was the immediate need. A wise man like Duncan Forbes of Culloden saw this, and he was as good a Highlander as Breadalbane, who wanted to turn the clans into a standing army in Government pay.

Eight months ago the financial scheme had been revived. There had been some curious by-play about the business at which he could only guess, for the chiefs themselves had been sounded as to the best negotiator. None would accept Argyll; Glengarry had wanted Atholl; but Lochiel had been strong for his cousin Breadalbane, and Breadalbane had been chosen. There had been a moment in the previous spring when the Government had leaned to severity, and he had been ordered by the Council forthwith to summon and disarm the clans and compel an oath of submission at the point of the sword. The order had been insane and he had protested, but he had duly issued the summons, and found that the "middle sort of people" everywhere were ready to submit. Lochiel, Keppoch, Clanranald, the Macleans and the Macintoshes, the men of Appin and Glencoe, all seemed to be in a yielding humour; only Sleat and Glengarry were proving difficult, and the latter had set about fortifying his house.

But presently he heard that the order was rescinded, and that Breadalbane was busy with his diplomacy. In the last days of June there was a conference at his castle of Achallader, which looked over Loch Tulla from under the shadow of the Glenlyon hills. Many of the chiefs were present, and the Jacobite leaders, Buchan and Barclay, and there a truce was signed to last till October 1. During that period there were to be no acts of hostility by either side on land or sea. There were also certain secret articles which provided that the truce was only to hold if James approved, and if there was no general rising, and that, if it fell through, Breadalbane was to rise for James with a thousand men.

Hill had got wind of the secret clauses and had duly sent them to Sir Thomas Livingstone, his official chief, while the Council received another copy from a nephew of Buchan. The result had been a furious row with Breadalbane, who was sore also at the failure of his bribery scheme. With that he had made no headway. The chiefs would not submit to be patronised by one whom they considered no better than themselves, and they distrusted his promises, believing that the London gold would never get beyond the vaults of Kilchurn. Hill's conscience in the matter was clear. Much as he disliked Breadalbane, he had done his best to help him, and had laboured to persuade Keppoch and Lochiel. But meantime the Government had followed up the Achallader truce. On the 27th of August 1691, there was issued at Edinburgh a proclamation pardoning and indemnifying all who had been in arms against the Government, provided that, before the first day of January 1692, they took the oath of allegiance before a sheriff or sheriff-depute.

Hill had not been fully convinced of the wisdom of the step. To ask within a period of five months the disavowal of the politics of a lifetime was to ask a good deal. He would have preferred to let Jacobitism as a sentiment die slowly away, but to keep a strict check on its armed manifestations. But his duty was to obey, and at any rate the Government seemed to have got a new vigour. Recalcitrants were to be firmly dealt with, and the regiments of Leven and of Buchan's Whig brother John were ordered to be ready for action.

At first he had been hopeful. In May there had been, as he had reported, a very genuine desire on the part of the clans to come in, except a few hot-heads. The Appin and Glencoe men had been willing to go to Inveraray, and take the oath before Argyll, their feudal superior, a marvellous concession for two most turbulent septs. Achtriachtan, one of the cadet gentry of Glencoe, and the tacksman of Inverrigan had made their submission and been given his protection early in November. The Government had been discreet, and had been faithful to the "gentle methods" which he had recommended. He had had trouble with Stewart of Appin, who had imprisoned one of his soldiers, and he had been compelled to arrest him and a son of Glencoe and bring them to Inverlochy, but they had been released on the Queen's special order.

But as the months passed he had been growing anxious. The honour of the Highlander had been touched, and no man would take the lead in renouncing ancient loyalties, especially as there were constant rumours of French fleets on the sea and of King James returning to his own. He had expected trouble with Sleat and the stubborn Glengarry, but the whole Highlands seemed to be in no mood to give in. It was now almost the end of December and few clans had signed. Lochiel, Glengarry, Keppoch, Appin had not sworn, and only a day or two remained .... That morning he had had word that Lochiel was starting for Inveraray. It was like the crooked Highland mind to deem it more honourable to postpone to the last moment an inevitable step.

Hill rose and walked to the window on the side away from the wind. The snow had stopped drifting, and the last gleam of daylight revealed beyond a rampart a shoulder of hill, a strip of leaden loch, and a low sullen sky. He shivered. There were months yet of winter before him, and his ague would assuredly return. What a God-forgotten country, and what a cruel fate for an old man to be marooned among these wilds! He thought of his daughters in London whom he never saw; he should be in the bosom of a family at his age, with a knighthood and a pension and a sinecure, instead of dwelling cold in the wilderness ....

And then — for the man's mind was just — he was a little ashamed of his humour. After all, he had position and respect, a roof to cover him and food to eat, which was more than could be said of some of James's men who had embraced beggary for a scruple. It was more than could be said of most of the clans, who every winter were on the verge of starvation. All round him the common folk looked white and peaked. To send soldiers, who had a bellyful of meat under their belts, against such scarecrows was scarcely decent .... To his surprise, as he looked over the darkening narrows of Loch Linnhe, he found himself a partisan of the Highlanders.

The truth was that he liked them, as Mackay had liked them. Mackay had always said that they were the best natural material for soldiers on earth, and he agreed with him. That made them a peril to the State, but some day it might make them a shining buckler. They had done famously at Killiecrankie, and at the worst they had been true to their salt. Moreover, they were friendly folk and well-mannered, and when they spoke English at all they spoke it intelligibly, and not like Angus's whiggamores, whom he had found wholly incomprehensible. They were noble companions in the chase or over a friendly bottle. For some of them, like Lochiel, he had a warm affection. Besides, he felt himself called upon to be their protector, for had he not known them for nearly forty years? His policy was Monk's rather than Mackay's; Monk had believed in a firm policing hand and with it patience, while Mackay had wanted to set a date for surrender and after that "to rouse them out of the nation as the bane thereof." He did not like that kind of language, though by it Mackay only meant burning their houses and crops; it was too like Breadalbane's talk of "mauling" them, which he suspected had a more sinister implication than Mackay's. The worst enemy of the Highlander might be other Highlanders.

Suppose their recalcitrance continued beyond the appointed day. Then there would be ugly work, since the troops would be loosed among the winter hills. There would be beyond question barbarities, and he was less afraid of Leven's and Buchan's Lowlanders than of his own men of Argyll's. In his recent letters there had been talk of wholesdale destruction. He comforted himself by reflecting that a great clan, like the Camerons or the Macdonalds, could not be destroyed; there would be some bitter fighting, and then, when the lesson had been learned, there would be peace.

Yes, but what of the lesser septs? The Appin Stewarts? They would not be an easy folk to shepherd, for they had the sea and the sea islands for a refuge. The Glencoe men? .... He pulled himself up sharply, for he realised that Glencoe was precisely the kind of case he dreaded.

The clan there was a branch of the Macdonalds, but cut off in a long chasm of a glen from their kinsmen. They were a small people, less that a quarter of the clans of Maclean or Sleat or Glengarry or Lochiel, less than half of Appin or Keppoch. But they could muster fifty fighting men in the field, and they were natural warriors. They had been at Killiecrankie and afterwards with Buchan and Cannon; they were Catholics, and staunch Jacobites, and ill regarded by the Government. They were cattle thieves like the rest, and unhappily their raids took them into the domains of potent and revengeful people like Argyll and Breadalbane. Argyll hated them because, like Appin, they formed a salient that jutted into his own territory. Breadalbane had all manner of ancient grudges against them, and in the June conference at Achallader he had had high words with their chief Maclan over an alleged theft of cows, and had threatened to do him a mischief — Hill had this direct from the chief's son.

He had long known Maclan — as a young man he had given Monk no trouble — and had liked him for his high spirit and good nature; no Highlander was better spoken of for fidelity to his word and courage in battle than that gigantic old man. He had liked, too, the second son, Alasdair, one of Buchan's captains, who for some time had been his prisoner at Inverlochy. He could not think happily of that little clan at the mercy of callous Lowland lawyers like Stair and ruthless intriguers like Breadalbane. Achtriachtan and Inverrigan had made their peace, but there was no word of any movement by the other Maclans.

The MacDonalds were cut off in a long chasm of a glen from their kinsmen.

The fools, the pitiful fools, when the sword of Democles hung above their heads!

Anxiety had driven out of Hill's mind his own grievances. This was a miserable business just when the Highlands were settling down. For months he had been writing to Livingstone and the Council that the whole district was peaceable and civil. Peaceable and civil — these had been his very words. Except for a little raiding in the Rough Bounds the land had been at ease. Yet in a month's time it might be in the throes of a bloody war. The best news he could get would be that every chief in Lochaber was posting to Inveraray or Inverness. Especially those stubborn fools of Glencoe, who were certain to be the first burnt-offering.

From his window he had a view of a corner of the barrack square, and the road from the main entrance. There seemed to be the stir of some arrival. In the gathering darkness he had a glimpse of a man dismounting from horseback. It could not be one of his patrols, for no patrol had gone out that day in the wild weather. It could not be his deputy Hamilton returning, for he was not expected back from the south yet awhile. He moved from the window as an orderly entered with a lamp, and behind him his major, Culloden's brother.

The latter's weather-beaten face was puckered in a grin. "Who do you think is here, sir?" he asked. "A penitent seeking mercy. No less than Glencoe himself!"

"Glencoe!" Hill cried. "Bring him here instantly. The very man I have had in my mind all afternoon."

Major Forbes ushered in a remarkable figure of a man. He was very tall, nearly six and a half feet, but so broadly made that his massiveness rather than his height was what first caught the eye. He had the wild dark eyes of Clan Donald, and a fierce nose like the beak of a galley. His white hair fell almost to his shoulders, and two great moustachios like buck's horns gave him the air of a Norse sea-king. His age was nearer seventy than sixty, but he held himself like a youth. In his bonnet was a bunch of faded heather, the Macdonald badge. He had trews of the dark tartan, and huge riding-boots of untanned leather, his broad belt carried a dirk and a brace of pistols, and at his side swung a long sword. He wore a fine buff coat, instead of the doublet of bull's hide for which he was famous. Hill knew the tale of that coat — it had been part of the plunder of Edinglassie, and had been often referred to in the processes of forfeiture against Dundee's followers .... He had not seen the man for thirty years. The Governor of Inverlochy reflected ruefully that age had dealt more kindly with this turbulent chieftain than with a docile servant of the law like himself.

The old man held up his right hand in salutation.

"It is Maclan," he said. "He has come to take the Government's oath."

"You have been too long about it," Hill replied drily, for his anxiety had made him irritable. "Why do you come here? You should be at Inveraray."

"You are the Governor of Inverlochy."

"I am a soldier, and the law ordains that the oath must be taken before a civil officer." He picked up a paper from the table. "These are the words of his Majesty's proclamation: —
'The persons who have been in arms before the time foresaid, and shall plead and take benefit of this our gracious indemnity, shall swear and sign the oath of allegiance to us by themselves, or the sheriff clerk subscribing for such as cannot write, and that before famous witnesses, betwixt and the first day of January next to come, in presence of the Lords of our Privy Council — or the sheriff — or their deputes — of the respective shires where any of the said persons live.'

"The words are explicit. Only a civil officer can swear you."

Hill spoke tartly, for this was an old grievance of his. He had often urged that the Governor of Inverlochy should have the powers of a civil magistrate, as he had had in Monk's day.

"Three months back you received Achtriachtan," the old man protested.

"I received Achtriachtan into the King's peace, and gave him a written protection, but I warned him that he had not fulfilled the law, and must go to Inveraray to complete his submission . You knew that, Maclan, you and your clan. In May last you were willing to go to Argyll at Inveraray, you and your cousins of Appin."

"That was in May," was the answer. "Since then I am not liking the name of Campbell. I was at Achallader in June and had ill words from the fox of Breadalbane." He spoke good English, with the soft lilting accent of the Gael.

Hill laughed. "I have been informed of that. My lord Breadalbane had somewhat against you in the matter of cattle-lifting."

Maclan drew himself up.

"There was talk of that, but it was a lawful act of war. After the death of the Graham, Coll of Keppoch and we of Glencoe, returning to our homes, drove a booty from Glenlyon who was an enemy of our King. Was that a greater fault than the killing of the red soldiers at Killiecrankie, for which your Government offers pardon?"

"That was not the first cause of offence given to my lord Breadalbane?"

Maclan's gravity broke into a smile.

"Maybe no. Glencoe has never loved Glenorchy — or Glenlyon, since Mad Colin hung thirty-six braw men of ours on the Meggernie braes. Maybe it is true that cattle beasts from Glenorchy have sometimes found themselves in Coire Gabhail, and that there has been some dirking of Campbells by Maclans. Gentlefolk will always be bickering if they live too near, and be gartering their hose tighter when the nights grow dark. But the Maclans have never wronged their neighbours as Breadalbane

Hill spelled out the seriousness of matters to Maclan

has, or by a coward's law pleas and dirty parchments stripped them of the lands they heired from their fathers."

"No. I never credited your clan with a taste for parchments. . . . But let us talk sense, for this is a grave business. You are within the danger of the law for your doings in the late rebellion. You have incurred the undying hatred of the most powerful folk in the Highlands, Argyll and Breadalbane. The King in his mercy offers you a way of peace. What do you do? First you come to the wrong place — to Inverlochy — to me, who can do nothing for you."

"I am a soldier, and would make my submission to a soldier."

"A plague upon your punctilios. I tell you, though I were Schomberg or Talmash I would be powerless. The law says a civil officer . . . Secondly, you put it off till the last moment. In two days it will be the New Year and the period of mercy will have closed. Was that not blind folly, with the menace of an offended Government hanging over you, and your good friends of Glenlyon and Glenorchy waiting for their revenge?"

The old man's face was troubled.

"I did only as others did. How many have sworn? Lochiel is but now gone to Inveraray."

"So you know that? But Lochiel is in a different case from you. He is the head of a big clan, and Argyll has always been his friend. Glengarry has not sworn, but he has a strong castle and is ill to come at. You are a little people, and you have no friends near by, and the great folk love you as a shepherd loves a fox, and you are so situate that Glencoe can be inclosed like a nut between crackers."

The other's eyes grew more troubled, but his voice was proud.

"As one fighting man to another so I speak to you, Colonel, and I will tell you the naked truth. I could not take my oath to your Government." (Hill noticed that he said 'Government' and never 'King' — for him there could be but the one king.) "Not till I was assured that a certain hope had gone. You say truly that we of Glencoe are a small people but we have had no traitors among us since the daughter of MacHenry first brought the clan to Glen Donald. The men of Ian Abrach draw their blood from Ian Og Fraoch, the son of that Angus Og who sheltered King Robert in his castle of Dunaverty in the south. Our race and our religion make us true to the lawful line of kings, and though we were to be swept from the earth we could not forswear that allegiance save by our King's order."

"That order is come?"

"Such is the word brought to me."

"Well, you are in the devil's own predicament. Loyalty is a high virtue, Maclan, though yours is a thought perverse. We were friends in youth and I would fain help you. I cannot receive you into the King's peace. You must get you to Inveraray, and you have two days to do it in. In this foul weather you may be hard put to it and be late for the fair. Have you any well-wishers there?"

"I have many ill-wishers, and the chief of them is MacCailein Mor himself."

"Argyll is not in the town at present, which is the better for you. Sir Colin Campbell is the sheriff-depute."

"Ardkinglas, though a Campbell, is an honest man," said the chief.

"I am happy to agree with you. He is also my friend, and I will write him a letter. Go straight to Ardkinglas and do not meddle with Duncanson the procurator-fiscal, for he has no good-will to any of your name."

Hill sat down at the table and took up his pen, reading aloud each sentence as he wrote it. He begged Ardkinglas to receive this 'lost sheep' who had misread his Majesty's proclamation and sought peace in the wrong quarter. Though Maclan were a day or two late — for the weather in Lochaber was severe — let a point be stretched and his submission be received. He subscribed himself his friend and well-wisher and colleague in the great task of peace-making.

As he sanded the ink he observed that Maclan had set his bonnet on his head and was rebuttoning his buff coat as if for instant departure. The chief took the letter, placed it in an inner pocket, and offered his hand. "May God and the saints have you in keeping," he said. "In two hours I must be beyond Loch Leven."

"Not so," said Hill. "Prayer and provender never yet hindered a man. You will sup with me — I have something better than the salted mart, for the last frigate brought certain Lowland delicacies, and you will sleep here. The wind is veering, and I think there will be no more snow."

He was wrong. At three in the morning when, by the light of a waning moon, Maclan mounted his shelty and, attended by his four running footmen, turned his face down Loch Linnhe, the wind still set icily from the north-west, and the snow was again falling. Hill, who in a greatcoat and nightcap saw him off, watched the little party disappear in the brume. "If he does not perish in a drift," he muttered to himself, "he will be a week late. God send that Ardkinglas be merciful!"

CHAPTER TWO
Inveraray and Edinburgh

Maclan and his gillies took the road down Loch Linnhe in a thick downfall of snow. The drifts were small, for the full force of the wind was cut off by the Ardgour hills. It was still black darkness when they reached the narrows of Loch Leven, and found on the beach the boat by which they had crossed the previous afternoon. Here, too, there was some shelter from the storm, and they made the passage without difficulty. Three

miles on the left a light twinkled. That came from Maclan's own
house of Carnoch at the foot of Glencoe, where his kin waited
anxiously to hear the result of his errand. One of the gillies was
sent off with a message, but he himself had no time to waste.
The quickest route to the south, had it been summer-time, was
up the Laroch stream, between Ben Vair, the 'Mountain of
Lightnings', and his own Meall Mor, and so by Glen Creran to
Connel ferry, but in this weather a fox or a deer could not have
made that journey. He turned to the right and took the shore
road through Appin.

Dawn came upon them near Duror, a dawn of furious
winds and solid driving snow. Happily it was a fine snow with
sleet in it, and so it did not greatly clog the path, but the force of
the gale was enough to lift a man off his feet. The running
gillies, bent double, their bonnets dragged over their brows,
their wet kilts plastered about their thighs, and their bare legs
purple with the cold, felt it less than the chief on his shelty. He
brought the folds of his plaid twice round his throat, but even so,
and for all his years of hardihood, he felt numbed and crippled
by the savagery of the heavens. Not a wild thing, bird or beast,
was stirring — they knew better; but he himself dare not seek
shelter, though the warm chimney-corner of Ardsheal awaited
him a mile off. For he knew that he was riding on a mission of
life and death. He tried to comfort his heart by reminding
himself that the great Montrose had travelled this very road at
the same time of year before that fight at Inverlochy when he set
the heather above the gale. But Montrose had had open
weather for his march, and the gale seemed now for good to
have overtopped the heather. *(The heather is the Macdonald
badge; the gale, or bog-myrtle, the Campbell.)*

They made slow progress, and midday found them no
further than Appin Kirk. At the inn of Creagan they had a dram
of hot whisky and a bite of bread and cheese. But the wind there
was so fierce that the ferryman dare not trust his coble on the

water, and they were compelled to go round by the head of Loch Creran, a circuit of several miles. Maclan's hope was to be beyond Loch Etive before nightfall — maybe even to reach the inn at Taynuilt under Cruachan. But with the afternoon the wind grew stronger and the snowfall more resolute, and it was almost dark when he reached Barcaldine, where the road turned south through Benderloch to the sea.

Whether he had desired it or not he had to halt at Barcaldine, for the road passed close to the castle, and half a dozen fellows in the Campbell tartan ran out to bar it. They recognised the old man, and their faces were not kind. Maclan knew the place too well, the keep, built long ago by Duncan of the Seven Castles, which commanded the shore road from Appin to Lorn. He cursed the fate which had brought him within its pale, for the Campbells of Barcaldine were near kin to Breadalbane, and one of them had been the companion of that fox when he carried war into Caithness.

As he had feared, the garrison was of Glenorchy men. Its

commander was a Captain Drummond, one of Breadalbane's Tayside neighbours, and the troops were of Argyll's regiment. Maclan presented Hill's letter, but at first Drummond would not read it. He had all the Lowland ill manners, so hateful to the Gael, who would use an enemy like a gentleman till he dirked him. The old man was treated half as spy and half as prisoner, given bare quarters and coarse food, and held under constant surveillance. He spent a night of anxiety and discomfort, but in the morning Drummond had relented. After all, he dare not offend Hill, for he and his men were under orders for the Inverlochy garrison. Maclan had something of a breakfast and was told that he might continue his journey, but it was not till the afternoon that his gillies were dug out from a noisome cellar, his shelty recovered, and a start made.

Twenty-four precious hours had been lost. Late that night the party reached Taynuilt, and as he got to bed Maclan heard a

In a second snowstorm they struggled up the Pass of Brander.

clock strike midnight. The New Year had begun and the time of probation was officially past.

Next day, in a second snowstorm, they struggled up the Pass of Brander beside a swollen river, and came to Loch Awe, scourged by a thousand blasts from the gullies of Cruachan. Never had he known such a blizzard. Five or six miles an hour were nothing to his long-limbed gillies, but now in an hour they could cover less than a mile. The snow was drifting too, and often they had to take to the rough hillside which the winds had swept bare. Darkness was on them before they had left the loch, and they spent the night in an empty sheiling. By the next morning, the second day of January, the storm had abated, and early that forenoon they dropped down Glen Aray to the little burgh which lay snug in the trench of its sea-loch.

Here Maclan had staggering news. He was two days late, and Ardkinglas, the sheriff-depute, was not there to receive him. Sir Colin had gone on a Hogmanay visit to kinsfolk, he was told, and had no doubt been storm-stayed.

For three wretched days the old man abode in Inveraray. Hill's letter was protection enough and he had been received respectfully by the sheriff's office, but the burgh was not a healthy place for his tartan, and, with half the people still festive from the Hogmanay revels, there would be a certainty of brawls if it were seen in the streets. So he and his men found quarters in an obscure hostelry, and stayed indoors all day, while Maclan morning and evening visited the sheriff's house to get news of the laggard Sir Colin. He was miserably anxious, for he saw that his delay had given a supreme chance to his enemies. If the sheriff stood on the letter of the law, as he was entitled to do, his estates were forfeit and he and his clan were broken men — nameless, landless, like the wretched Macgregors. Ill-omened memories came to haunt him. A spaewife had prophesied that he would be murdered in his own house. He was resolved that that house should not see him again till he returned to it with the Government pardon in his pocket.

On the third day — the fifth of January — Sir Colin came back to town, rosy from his travels. He was a just man, whose patriotism was for all the Highlands and not merely for his clan, and he earnestly desired peace. He read Hill's letter and read it again, and knit his brows. For he was in a quandary. Maclan had missed his chance, and the law should take its course; he had no power to extend the period laid down in the King's proclamation. But if he refused to receive him, Maclan's life would be forfeit, for he was aware of the hounds waiting to be unleashed, and he had an honest man's tenderness for one whom he knew to be an honest foe.

"What makes you so dooms behindhand?" he asked, and was told the storm and the detention at Barcaldine — not to mention the initial mistake of the bootless errand to Inverlochy.

"Well, you're in a fine creel. I see nothing for it but that I should decline to give you the oath. The thing's clean beyond my power."

The old man, knowing that here was no enemy, but a perplexed friend, humbled his pride and begged for mercy. He even wept, he whose eyes were not used to tears. Let him be permittted to take the oath, he said, and every man of his clan would do the like; if any refused, he would be sent to prison or impressed for the Flanders wars. Sir Colin was moved, and finally persuaded.

"Come back the morn," he said, "and I'll see what can be done for you."

When Maclan returned on the 6th of January, the sheriff-depute had made up his mind. "I'll swear you," he said, "but, mind, I cannot guarantee that the thing is in order. Our sheriff-clerk is in Edinburgh, and I will send the certificate to him, and get him to take the opinion of the Council on the matter. Not that I think they will quarrel with what I have done, for no more than me do they want further dispeace in the Highlands. Likewise I will write a letter to Colonel Hill, asking him to give you and yours full interim protection. That is the best I can do for you, Maclan, but I think it will suffice. It is not likely that the Council will question my judgment. You can sleep sound in your bed in yon fearsome black glen of yours."

That afternoon in better weather the chief departed thankfully from the town of Inveraray, which seemed to his mountain eyes part miracle and part prison. He had no fear for his safety. The Campbell word was law now in the land, and in Argyll Sir Colin was the second greatest Campbell.

After his departure Ardkinglas, according to his promise, wrote to his namesake Colin Campbell, the sheriff-clerk of Argyll, now in Edinburgh, enclosing the certificate of Maclan's submission and asking that it should be declared by the Council to be in order. He also wrote to the Governor of Inverlochy commending Glencoe to his protection, but for some reason omitted to send off the letter for three days. But one important missive he despatched at once by a special messenger. He sent an account of the whole busines to his chief Argyll in London.

The further history of Maclan's oath is obscure. The Scottish Privy Council in that month of January was not greatly interested in the pacification of the clans; to it, and to William, a more urgent matter was the coming General Assembly of the Kirk and what might be the policy of the Presbyterian hot-heads. The certificate duly reached the hands of the sheriff-clerk in Edinburgh, who took it to the clerks of the Council, Sir Gilbert Elliot, the founder of the Minto family, and Mr David Moncrieff. They naturally refused to receive it, since the time limit had expired. Thereupon the sheriff-clerk, along with Mr John Campbell, a Writer to the Signet, took the opinion of a Lord of Session, Lord Aberuchill, also a Campbell. There seems to have been no question of clan bias, for these Campbells may be presumed to have been anxious to do Ardkinglas's will. Aberuchill, who was a member of the Privy Council, put the matter before several of his colleagues, one of whom was the new Lord Stair, the father of Sir John Dalrymple. They gave it as their view that the certificate could not be accepted without a special warrant from the King, and accordingly it was scored through and cancelled.

The matter was never brought before the Council as a whole, though such had been Ardkinglas's intention, for there was no need of that if good legal opinion held that the Council had no power to extend the time. We need not suspect malign Dalrymple influence, for the decision was on the face of it sound law; the Proclamation of August 27 permitted the oath to be taken before the Lords of the Council as well as before the sheriffs, but gave neither of these parties any power to vary its conditions.

It is more difficult to explain why the matter was not referred to London and the King's pleasure taken. The probable reason was that before this could be done — for the wheels of Scottish justice moved slow — word came that the fate of Maclan had already been decided. For the next stage of the drama we must turn to the south.

CHAPTER THREE

Kensington

A chief actor must now be introduced on the stage. The day is the 11th of January in the year 1692. The scene is the palace of Kensington, which William had bought from Lord Nottingham and made his chief dwelling, because he found Whitehall bad for his asthma and Hampton Court too remote from London.

A man sat in a warm wainscoted room with a table of papers before him. He congratulated himself that in this wintry weather his business with the King gave him quarters in the palace, so that he was not compelled to jog twice a day along the miry footpad-haunted roads which linked Kensington village with the capital. Now and then he cast a glance from the window at the new Dutch garden in which workmen were busy, and thought that he might well borrow a hint from it for his own Galloway home of Castle Kennedy. But chiefly he kept his eyes on his papers, for he had much troublesome business on hand.

The occupant of the chair was a handsome full-bodied man in his forty-fourth year. Sir John Dalrymple, now Master of Stair, was a figure not easily forgotten. The face framed in the huge perruque was immensely intelligent. The eyes under the broad brow were cool, wary and commanding. The lips were full but compressed, there was humour at the corners of the mouth, and the heavy jowl had a jovial, almost porcine, air. Yet the impression left upon the spectator was not that of geniality, but of a mocking competence, an almost arrogant self-complacency. And something more — something subtle and tortuous, a warning that this man would not be easily fathomed, and might be an uncertain colleague and a precarious friend. The seventeenth-century chroniclers were fond of finding 'aliquid insigne' in their characters' faces — Sir Philip Warwick found it in the Duke of Hamilton's, and Clarendon in the younger Vane's. This something extraordinary was beyond doubt in the mobile countenance of the man in the chair.

He came of a strange family. His father, Sir James, the first Viscount Stair, had raised himself from a small Ayrshire lairdship to the peerage, the repute of the greatest Scots lawyer of the day, and a share in the inner councils of the King. He had been many things in his time — soldier, professor, advocate, lord of Session; he had quarrelled first with Lauderdale and then with Claverhouse; though no fanatic he had tried to protect the Covenenters, and had been for some years an exile in Holland before he returned with William. He had written on religion and on the law — on the latter so profoundly that he still ranks as the greatest institutional jurist of his country. His ability all men admired, but few trusted him and fewer liked him. There was something uncanny about him and his race; he had a masterful wife whose piety did not save her from charges of dabbling in forbidden arts; fate seemed to brood over the house of Stair as it shadowed the house of Atreus, and a daughter and a grandson were the centre of tragic tales.

The son's life had been not less chequered than the father's. He had been more than once in prison, and had often gone in danger of his head. He had been Claverhouse's bitter enemy, yet he had become James's Lord Advocate, and had been responsible for the prosecution of James Renwick, the last martyr of the Covenant. He had taken the chief part in offering the crown of Scotland to William, and had had the difficult task of managing William's business in the first Scottish parliaments. Now, with the King often abroad at the wars, he was the virtual ruler of Scotland, for his colleague in the north, Johnston of Wariston, was a trivial being. He had as few friends as his father, and far more avowed enemies, since the Jacobites hated him as a turncoat, and the extreme Presbyterians as a trimmer and a Laodicean. He admitted the second charge, for if there was one thing he detested it was high-flying religion. As to the first, his,defence was that he had served James only to prepare the way for the inevitable revolution, since he had always been William's man. He flattered himself that he had been a consistent Whig.

The man was not all of one piece. He had a human side known to his few intimates. In private life he was notably good-natured, and his conversation was full-flavoured and merry. Sometimes in debate his dignity would break down, and he would scold an opponent like a fishwife. But the figure he presented in public affairs was clean-cut, impregnable, and highly unsympathetic, for alone of Scottish statesmen he had a policy, and the determination to enforce it. Let us try to set down the ideas at the back of his head.

The Master of Stair would scold an opponent like a fishwife.

He had his father's legal mind, but he was several stages further off than his father from the turbid old Scots world of fevered beliefs and unprofitable loyalties. He was emphatically the man of a new age, with something of the same outlook as Somers and Halifax. He sought order and reason and civilisation, and he hated all that he believed to stand in the way of these blessings. They were his faith, though he was sceptical about most things.

For a sentimental Jacobitism he had only scorn, and of religious fanaticism he was wholly intolerant. He honestly desired that Scotland should settle down into reputable ways, when her citizens should be secure in life and goods, and could advance from their present grinding poverty to the prosperity which he believed to be within their compass. He remembered too bitterly what had happened before the Revolution to wish to see that anarchy perpetuated.

Also, for he was a statesman with a wide vision, he saw the needle-point upon which Britain stood. A litlle laxness here, a blunder there, would shiver the brittle framework of peace. Jacobitism was still a cave of Adullam to which might resort the multitudinous forces of discontent. Quiet at home was the first essential, for William, of whom he was the loyal servant, was fighting a desperate battle — how desperate was only known to a man like him who had lived with the King in his Flanders camps. He was opposing with weak allies the greatest monarch and the most formidable confederation in the world. He had to face Luxemburg, the little, harsh-featured hunchback who was the foremost military genius of the day, the greatest general produced by the house of Montmorency; a brilliant second in Boufflers; and a sagacious war minister in Louvois. Ireland was for the moment quiescent, but the continental campaign of 1691 had been a failure, with the loss of Mons and the defeat at Leuse, and the omens were not bright for the new year. It was his business to see that no folly at home crippled the force of the British stroke beyond the Channel.

The Master of Stair was a Lowlander with most of the merits and every defect of that stalwart breed. The virtues which he respected were order, sobriety, prudence, industry; he had no taste for the romantic glories and little patience with them. His blood was cool and his imagination strictly disciplined. Not only was he a Lowlander, but he was a son of that south-west region of Scotland where the Lowland qualities of individualism and independence were found in their most truculent form. Small as his liking had been for the Covenant, he had tried to protect the Covenanters, realising that, though in a temporarily perverted form, they had the virtues which might make the kind of citizens he desired to see. Therefore he was utterly impatient with those who preferred a romantic whimsy to common sense, and with all the sentimental rodomontade for which his old enemy Claverhouse had died. If Scotland was ever to become a civilised land it must get rid of this lumber of the middle ages.

Above all he was intolerant of the Highlands. It shocked his orderly mind that one half of Scotland should be as barbarous as the wilds of America. He had to the full the Lowland hatred and fear of those northern mists from which time and again had come banditti to trouble the peace of Scotland. The Highlands were the home of a clan system which was half autocratic and half communal, and in both respects hateful to a Whig. They were the last refuge of Jacobitism. The life was barbarous and brutal, and the King's writ ran limpingly. There lay the danger-point, and if the peril was to be crushed it must be done at once, for the present police force, Leven's and Argyll's regiments, would soon be required in Flanders. He had never crossed the Highland line, but he had met Highlanders, and he liked them little — Glengarry, Lochiel, Appin and the rest of them, huge, flamboyant, witless bravos.

Fortunately there were some few Highlanders who were on the side of common sense. Tarbat was one; he had no great love for Tarbat, but at any rate he talked the language of educated men and he knew on which side his bread was buttered. Argyll, too; a trumpery creature, but his interests were now solid for the Government. Breadalbane — and at the thought of Breadalbane the Master lay back in his chair and pondered. This was the hardest nut of all to crack, and the most important in the platter.

The man was in town. He had come up at Christmas to report. He had been at the palace that very morning. Breadalbane's face rose before Dalrymple, for in his sleeping and waking hours it was a constant enigma to him; and well it might be, for the face as it looks at us from the canvas of Sir John Medina seems to have been formed to conceal the soul behind it. It has the gravity of a Roman senator and the proud stateliness of a Spanish hidalgo; the mouth is steadfast and not unkindly, the eyes under the heavy lids have a sober dignity. Dalrymple flattered himself that he had no illusions about Breadalbane. He knew his past in all its shamelessness, a past of money-lending, blackmail, oppression, chicanery, and, when the need arose, of violence and murder. He knew that to the core he was avaricious and selfish, with no higher thought than his money-bags and his rent-rolls. He was aware that he had been deep in many treasons, and even now was suspected on good evidence of having intrigued in the summer on James's behalf with the Highland chiefs. He knew that he was the most comprehensively distrusted man in all Scotland.

But there was much to be said on the other side. No one denied his remarkable abilities. After Argyll he could bring more men into the field than any Highland grandee. And, like Dalrymple, he wanted peace. It stood to reason that he did, for his great domains, which stretched from Loch Awe to the haughs of Tay, were especially at the mercy of disorder. Behind him were the savage clans of Lochaber who loathed the name of Campbell, and had a readier access to his lands than they had to Argyll's. A settlement of the Highlands would enable him to reap in comfort what he had sown through fifty disreputable years. William could offer him more than James, for if the Stuarts returned it would be Glengarry and Sleat and Clanranald who would be in favour, not Breadalbane, however much he might have contributed to that return.

Besides, he had a policy. Breadalbane knew his

countrymen and had no doubt about the proper course. He had done his best with the scheme of bribing the clans, but that had failed. He had not opposed the King's proclamation of August. But he had been very clear about what the next step should be, if submission did not follow. The next proclamation must be written with a sharp pen and bloody ink. "Mauling" was his phrase; the recalcitrants must be so handsomely mauled that their will to resist would be crushed for ever. All the rebels, if possible, but if not, a selected few like Keppoch and Glencoe as an example. He had argued his case brilliantly, and Dalrymple had been convinced, for this man knew the nature of the Gael.

Yet as he lay back in his chair he was not quite at ease on the point. After all, the man had been one of the leaders of the Highland host which ten years ago had descended upon his own westlands. It was odd company for a Whig to find himself in. He had staked a good deal on Breadalbane and his nicely calculated honesty. He had written him letters which might some day be brought up against him. That day a Highland policy must be determined on, and he was still in two minds. There was a long *dossier* on the subject, and he must refresh his memory about the past. From a drawer in his table he took a bundle of papers, for he was a careful man and made his secretary copy every letter of importance to which he put his name.

Eight months ago he had been sanguine that the King's law could be brought to the Highlands without further bloodshed. He hated war — it was not his business, and he did not understand it, and he most earnestly desired a peaceful settlement. He had flung himself heart and soul into Tarbat's scheme of bribing the chiefs, and, because Breadalbane seemed the best agent, he had laid himself out to conciliate Breadalbane. How many letters had he not indited to him last summer from those comfortless Flanders camps! On June 25th he had written to encourage him in his negotiations. "If they wil be mad, before Lammas they will repent it, for the army will be allowed to go into the Highlands, which some thirst so much for, and the frigates will attack them; but I have so much confidence of your character and capacity to let them see the ground they stand on, that I think these suppositions are vain." A month later he had begged Breadalbane to get the clans to meet him in Edinburgh, and in the meantime he had been warning Livingstone that no acts of hostility should be committed against the Highlanders.

On September 28 from Loo he had encouraged Breadalbane to persevere in the good work, and urged that nothing should be done to exacerbate Highland feeling by undue suspicion. "The best cure of all these matters is, that the chieftains do it (take the oath) as quickly as can be, which will take off the trials or suspicions against the rest." Two days later he told him that he had spoken to the King about the money required, which would be forthcoming when needed, and reiterated his belief in his honesty, which so many were doubting. "The best evidence of sincerity," he had written, "is the bringing the matter quickly to a conclusion . . . . I hope your lordship shall not only keep them (the clans) from giving any offence, but bring them to take the allegiance which they ought to do very cheerfully, for their lives and fortunes they have from their Majesties."

The Master raised his head and considered. His conscience was clear. Never had man been more earnest in the cause of peace.

He turned the pages of the file and was reminded how in early December his hopes had begun to wane. There was a brief letter to Hamilton, Hill's second-in-command at Inver-lochy, warning him that the garrison might have to take the field on a punitive expedition, "for the winter-time is the only season in which we are sure the Highlanders cannot escape us, nor carry their wives, bairns and cattle to the mountains." The bribery plan had failed, and the clans showed no signs of obeying the King's proclamation of August. He was back in London then, and closer in touch with home affairs, and it looked as if nothing remained but a winter expedition. There must be no delaying after the day of grace, January 1, was past, for the regiments of Leven and Argyll would soon be due for Flanders.

To Breadalbane he wrote on December 2 that he thought Clan Donald should be rooted out, and his "doited cousin" Lochiel. As for the rumours about Breadalbane's own conduct, he had discussed them with the King, who treated them as trifles . . . . He had not quite given up hope, for next day he wrote again to Breadalbane with the news that Tarbat had had letters from Glengarry, and had seen William, who had gone carefully into the proposed payments to the different chiefs. "By the next I expect to hear either that these people are come to your hand, or else your scheme for mauling them, for it will not delay . . . . I am not changed as to the expediency of doing things by the easiest means and at leisure, but the madness of these people and their ungratefulness to you makes me plainly see that there is no reckoning on them, but *delenda est Carthago.* Yet who have accepted, and do take the oath, will be safe, but deserve no kindness . . . . Therefore look on and you shall be satisfied of your revenge."

The Master re-read the last letter, and with it another of the same date to Hamilton at Inverlochy. To the latter he had written: "Let me hear from you with the first whether you think that this is the proper season to maul them in the cold long nights, and what force will be necessary," and he added that he had written to the same purpose to Colonel Hill. Since the clans were apparently not coming in, it was very necessary to strike hard as soon as the new year began. Argyll's regiment was at Inverlochy, Leven's was at Inverness, and Buchan's (John the rubicund Whig, not his brother Thomas the sallow, saturnine Jacobite) was under notice to join it. What was in his mind was a brief vigorous campaign of mauling — "letters of fire and sword" in the old Scots phrase — the burning of hovels and stores, the driving away of cattle, and, when they resisted, the slaughter of men. It would be directed chiefly against Glengarry and his Macdonalds — "That's the only Popish clan in the kingdom, and it will be popular to take severe courses with them." This had always been Breadalbane's advice, and Breadalbane knew his countrymen.

There came a gap in the correspondence during the Christmas and New Year season, since Tarbat and Argyll and Breadalbane were all in London. For the first week of January 1692 the old plan stood. Here was his letter of the 7th to Livingstone, the Scottish commander-in-chief, informing him that orders would go out next day. It should be a short and sharp business. These were his words: "You know in general that those troops posted at Inverness and Inverlochy will be ordered to take in the house of Invergarry, and to destroy entirely the county of Lochaber, Lochiel's lands, Keppoch's, Glengarry's, Appin and Glencoe. If there be any opposition the troops (that is Leven's and Buchan's regiments) will need to join; if not, they may act separately, which will make the work the shorter. I assure you their power shall be full enough, and I hope the soldiers will not trouble the Government with prisoners. The slighting the offered mercy, and depending still upon foreign assistance, will justify all the severity which can be used against those who can neither be obliged nor trusted . . . . It's true, it's a rigid season for the soldiers to work, but it's the only time they cannot escape you, for human constitutions cannot endure to be now long out of houses. A few days will do all that's at present either necessary or possible."

The Master with his quill underlined these sentences. They seemed to him sound common sense. He was a convert to Breadalbane's view, the need of blood and iron. But in moderation. He had always prided himself upon being a moderate and humane man. A sharp lesson, after ample warning, would save much suffering in the future, and might bring to reason the chiefs who were now gambling with the lives of their wretched peoples. His policy was not extirpation — you could not extirpate the Macdonalds and the Camerons in a few days — but punishment.

A good policy, but now, alas! impossible. For the very next day had come news that the clans, after procrastinating to the last moment, had taken the oath. Lochiel and Appin had sworn at Inveraray — Glencoe too, so Hill reported; and Keppoch at Inverness; only Glengarry stood out. The whole plan of the punitive campaign had miscarried; all that remained was to deal with Glengarry and his fortified castle, and a troublesome little expedition like that would have no solemnising effect upon the Highland mind. On the 9th he wrote to Livingstone: "For my part I could have wished the Macdonalds had not divided, and I am sorry that Keppoch and Maclan of Glencoe are safe ... I would be as tender of blood or severities as any man, if I did not see the reputation of the Government in question upon slighted mercy, and the security of the nation in danger by those who have been obstinate to that degree that, if we believe them rational, we must think they depend upon such assurances of help that we can never oblige them even to their own advantages from this Government, and therefore it must make sure of them."

The Master restored the bundle of papers to its drawer, and turned to the letter he had begun to write. He had seen the King and was sending his instructions to Livingstone about the expedition against the few remaining recalcitrants. The Macleans in Mull, about whom there was some doubt, would be left to Argyll. Sleat, who was also doubtful, was to be dealt with. Glengarry, about whom there was no doubt, was to be attacked and Invergarry taken. William's inclinations were mild. Rebel chiefs were to be given quarter, and the commonalty, if they took the oath, were to be assured in their lives and property. In the covering letter to Livingstone the Master was emphasising this mercifulness. "I am most concerned," he wrote, "for the poor commonalty. I do well know, if nothing be done to disable them, they will join with their lairds and chieftains whenever these appear . . . . I think they should have some ease and feel the advantage of having the King their master . . . ."

He broke off to reflect upon his deep dissatisfaction with the whole business. There had been a general taking of the oath, but it had been insolently and defiantly put off till the eleventh hour. Glengarry might be punished, but that gave no security for peace, since nothing would have been done to change the Highland mind, no swift dramatic judgment, such as Breadalbane had always pled for, which would awe those barbarous but impressionable souls . . . .

A servant announced that the Earl of Argyll desired to see him. Argyll might throw more light upon the business. The Master had no belief in Argyll, either in his brains or in his character; his prominent shifting eyes were an advertisement of his instability to all the world. But Argyll had means of getting news which never entered the official flying packets.

He resumed his letter to Livingstone with a fateful sentence. "Just now my lord Argyll tells me that Glencoe hath not taken the oath, at which I rejoice. It's a good work of charity to be exact in rooting out that damnable sept — the worst in all the Highlands." Ardkinglas's despatch to his chief had brought the news that, though Maclan had sworn, it had been six days too late. He was still within the law's danger.

During the next few days there were many consultations between the Master, Argyll and Breadalbane, and several interviews with the King. On the 16th William signed additional instructions to Livingstone, which concluded thus: "If Maclan of Glencoe, and that tribe, can be well separated from the rest, it will be a proper vindication of the public justice to extirpate that sept of thieves."

*Consultations took place with the King
involving the Master, Argyll and Breadalbane.*

That day the Master wrote to Livingstone telling him that
the King would only receive recalcitrants now "on mercy", a
reference to Glengarry; but "for a just example of vengeance I
entreat this thieving tribe in Glencoe to be rooted out in
earnest." To Hill he wrote on the same day in the same terms,
but with an ominous addition. "The Earls of Argyll and
Breadalbane have promised they shall have no retreat in their
bounds. The passes to Rannoch would be secured, and the
hazard certified to the laird of Weem to retreat them. In that
case Argyll's detachment, with a party that may be posted in

Island Stalker, must cut them off." On the 30th he told Livingstone: "I am glad that Glencoe did not come in within the time prescribed. I hope what's done may be in earnest, since the rest are not in a condition to draw together to help. I think to herry their cattle or burn their houses is but to render them desperate, lawless men, to rob their neighbours; but I believe you will be satisfied it were a great advantage to the nation that thieving tribes were rooted out and cut off. It must be quietly done, otherwise they will make shift for both the men and their cattle." To Hill, also on the 30th, he wrote: "When anything concerning Glencoe is resolved, let it be secret and sudden." And on the 23rd Livingstone had written to Hamilton telling him that he and the Inverlochy garrison would be judged according to how they handled Glencoe. The Court, he added, rejoiced that Maclan had not taken the oath in time, "so that the thieving nest might be entirely rooted out."

Argyll's news had given the Master a new policy. He now saw a chance for a dramatic stroke which would carry terror to every rebellious heart. In Scotland commissions of fire and sword had been frequent shot for the rusty blunderbuss of criminal justice, and as a learned lawyer he knew all about them. To "destroy by fire and sword" was the common style of proclamation against "intercommuned rebels." That treatment had long ago been meted out to the Macgregor clan. In 1640 Argyll, the famous Marquis, had been given such a commission against the Atholl and Ogilvy lands. The words had a specific meaning, and to "extirpate" did not mean to exterminate, but at the worst only to make a clan landless and chiefless. The attack was usually made by day and in summer, and involved burning of crops and houses and driving of cattle, but as a rule little loss of life. This was how the Master intended the Macleans to be handled by Argyll, and Glengarry by the Inverlochy and Inverness garrisons.

But as for the Maclans, he meant extermination. He wanted a spectacular punishment, and this seemed a chance for it. It would need an army to exterminate great clans like Glengarry's and Lochiel's, dwelling over a wide stretch of country; even Keppoch, with open boundaries, would be hard to manage. But the Maclans in their ravine of Glencoe were a simpler matter. If the passes at either end were netted not a soul need escape.

How came this savage notion to dominate the mind of a politic and not inhumane statesman? The answer must be that he got it from Breadalbane and Argyll — but principally from Breadalbane. He wanted an exemplary sacrifice, and Breadalbane showed him where to find it. The Master himself knew less about Glencoe than he knew about the passes of the Alps. He disliked the clan because he had been told that they had been among the chief obstacles to the bribing policy of the previous summer, and that they were bitter Jacobites and notorious caterans even beyond the average Highlander. Breadalbane told him these things. He also pointed out that the physical nature of Glencoe made the place a trap which could be set and watched by a handful of troops. No need to trouble about Leven's and Buchan's regiments. He painted the Maclans as a blot upon the Highlands, a mere rabble of vermin, a disconsidered sept of Clan Donald whom even the other Jacobite clans would not study to avenge. His hatred and his local knowledge made his arguments weighty, and when he showed how he and Argyll could block the bolt-holes the Master was convinced. If we need further evidence for Breadalbane's part, we may note the fact that the executants of the tragedy were mostly his creatures, and that an evil conscience brought his steward to Glencoe after the massacre to try to buy the silence of the survivors.

The Master has come down to history with a heavy weight of blood-guilt upon him, and, even if Breadalbane's crime was the more heinous, it is hard to say that his condemnation is undeserved. He chose to depart from the standards of the civilisation which he preached, partly because he allowed a consideration of policy to over-ride the human decencies, partly because he regarded the Highlands, and especially the Maclans, as something less than human. It should be observed that barbarous cruelty, the slaying of young and old, man and woman and child, is not the only charge, for the scheme involved treachery, though he may have had no inkling of the deeps to which that treachery was to descend. A man of his intelligence cannot have been ignorant that treachery was inevitable if his instructions were carried out to do the thing "quietly" and to be "secret and sudden." He knew that the Maclans were living in fancied security, believing that Ardkinglas's acceptance of their oath had satisfied the law. Any sudden assault would be upon trusting and unsuspecting men. Having willed the end, he had willed also the unholy means.

How shall we apportion William's share? I find it impossible to believe that he was not a consenting party to the plan of wholesale murder. He knew nothing of the Scots practice of "fire and sword", and the mild interpretation given to the word "extirpate"; to him it must have borne its literal meaning. The main instructions he countersigned at the top as well as at the bottom, as if to give them special authority, which weakens Burnet's plea that he signed the document without reading it.

It is clear from the correspondence that he went meticulously into the business of the payments to the chiefs, and that the Master of Stair communicated to him every step he took. He heard that Maclan had taken the oath, though late; he knew that Glengarry, who had not sworn at all, was to be mercifully treated; but he approved of the extermination of the liittle clan of Glencoe as a politic expedient.

The fact that he did not punish the principal malefactors

when the truth became known is another proof that he felt that he was deeply implicated, for he was a man who was always honest with himself. Technically he carried the chief responsibility, for the measure was a military act, and Hamilton and Livingstone were not responsible to the Secretary for Scotland but to the King.

There is much to be said in extenuation. He knew nothing of the Highlands, and regarded Glencoe as a mere robbers' den. He was engaged in a life-and-death struggle, and had small leisure to inform himself about what he considered the uncouth barbarians of the north. He had no love for Scotland, and respected no Scotsmen but Carstares and the Dalrymples, and he may well have thought the blotting out of a few hundreds of its people to be no very serious matter. He was a great man, but neither humane nor gracious.

The burden of the scheme framed at Kensington in the latter half of January must rest upon three men, Breadalbane, the Master, and the King. The first has the heaviest share, the last the lightest. The guilt varies with the degree of knowledge, and the intimacy of the relationship between the wronged and the wronger. In William it was a crime against humanity in general, in the Master of Stair against his fellow Scots, and in Breadalbane against those who shared with him the blood and traditions of the Gael.

CHAPTER FOUR
Glencoe

Glencoe is a gash like a sword-cut among the loftiest and wildest of the Highland hills. At the western end of the Moor of Rannoch stand the sentinel Shepherds of Etive, and from their corries streams combine to form the infant Etive, which flows south-west to the sea-loch of that name, with on its left bank the *massif* of the Black Mount. North of the Shepherds the waters drain westward, and presently descend into a deep-cut glen, which stretches to Loch Leven. The northern wall is the long ridge of Aonach Eagach, the "Notched Hill"; its south the two Shepherds, the Buachaille Etive Mor and the Buachaille Etive Bheag; and then, going westward, the great bulk of Bidean nam Bian, the highest mountain in Argyll, till the ridge bends northward and sinks to the sea at Meall Mor.

The natural outlets are at the west, or sea end, towards Ballachulish, and in the east to the inn of Kingshouse, whence the traveller can make his way to Rannoch and Lochaber, or south to Glenorchy and the Breadalbane country. In the nine miles of its length the glen has few entries on its flanks. There is no gap in the northern wall of Aonach Eagach save the old military road, which climbs by the Devil's Staircase towards Kinlochleven and Mamore. On the south side, beginning from the east, there is the pass called the Lairig Gartain, leading between the two Shepherds to Glen Etive. After that there are only chimneys for the cragsman, till, on the north-west side of Bidean nam Bian, the two glens of Fionn and Bhuidhe provide difficult routes to Glen Etive and Glen Creran. In all the Highlands there is no other such well-defended sanctuary.

Down in the valley bottom the river Coe, after leaving the bleak moorlands of its birth, runs in deep linns between buttresses of crag, till, midway in its course, it expands into the

shallow and boggy Loch Triachtan. On the shelf north of the
loch stood at that time the village of Achtriachtan, with the
house of one of the cadet gentry of the clan. Thence it flows
through natural woodlands, receiving on its left the main
tributary from the corries of Bidean nam Bian. Just north of the
point of junction stood another village, Achnacon, and a little
further down the hamlet and farm of Inverrigan. The sea is now
in sight, and among dunes and woodlands, some natural and
some planted, stood the house of Carnoch, the principal house
in the glen and the residence of the chief. The clan, apart from
outlying shepherds' bothies and the high sheilings of the
summer-time, lived around Carnoch, and in the three clachans
of Achtriachtan, Inverrigan and Achnacon.

The marvels of the glen have been the theme of much
prose and verse. Looking down it from the east in wild weather
it can appear like some prison-house of the *Inferno,* but from
the same standpoint, when the sun is sinking beyond Ardgour
and the peaks are rose and gold above its purple abyss, it may
seem a gateway to happy enchantments. The quartzite and
schist formation, seamed by broad belts of porphyry, has
contorted the rocks into fantastic shapes, which are grim or fairy-
like according to the light and the weather. I know no landscape
so capricious in its moods. I have sat on a crag of Aonach Dubh
and peered down through driving snow into what seemed to be
a hyperborean hell; and I have looked up the glen on a June
evening, when the hills drowsed in a haze like sloeberry bloom
and the clear streams crooned among flowers and grasses, so
that the place seemed, in Neil Munro's words, one of the
"blessed corries, so endowed since the days when the gods
dwelt in them without tartan or spear, in the years of peace that
had no beginning."

The savagery was only in the hills, for Glencoe itself was a
fruitful and habitable place. There were juicy pastures by the
stream and on the shelves of the two Shepherds, where black
cattle could feed, and sheep and goats, and the ewe-milkers

were busy on the summer mornings. It was sheltered from the north and east winds, and its winters were mild. Loch Leven and Loch Linnhe gave its people herring and salmon, and the Coe was famous for its sea-trout. Oats and bear did well in the lower haughs. The hills were the haunt of the red deer, and the hazel coverts of roebuck, and the ancient royal Forest of Dalness was part of Maclan's territory and tenanted by a clansman. It is clear that Glencoe had a name not for bleakness but for snugness and comfort. "This countrie is verie profitable, fertill," wrote the seventeenth-century topographer, "plenteous of corne, milk, butter, cheese and abundance of fish." "A beautiful valley," wrote the author of the *Memoirs of Locheill*, and the eighteenth-century report was "a glen so narrow, so warm, so fertile . . . a place of great plenty and security." It was a "garden enclosed" as contrasted with the stony uplands of Knoydart or Mamore.

The life of the little clan that dwelt there was not the idyllic thing which some enthusiasts would have us picture it, but no more was it the naked barbarism of current Lowland belief. The Maclans had their own type of civilisation, their own economy, religion and laws. They were of the old faith, though it is not likely that a priest came often to celebrate mass in Glencoe. They were reported among their neighbours to be "very resolute, hardy, and stout, and to have the least vanity of any of the septs of Clan Donald." The society was patriarchal, the chief being the protector of his people, and also the judge, in which duty he had behind him a great mass of ancient traditional law. No fault was ever found with Maclan on these scores. Their economy was rudimentary but by no means barbarous. They grew their own corn, which sufficed except in a season of dearth. In summer and autumn hunting gave them ample store of game and fish. For the winter cattle were salted down, and salmon kippered. The herring gabbarts from the Clyde brought them Lowland manufactured goods to be exchanged for their fish and skins. The surplus of the black cattle was sent south in droves to the Lowland fairs. A certain amount of money circulated, and luxuries were not unknown; there was a smattering of education, and many could talk English and a little French.

Normally their life was peaceful, but now and then the crops would fail, the cattle could get no winter fodder, and after the ancient fashion the young men would go out to drive a prey from the lands of ancestral enemies. Behind all these raids, whether in Argyll or Breadalbane or further afield, there was always, it should be remembered, a sense of getting back that of which they had been unlawfully deprived. Sometimes, too, there was a matter of personal revenge, reprisals when there was no hope of otherwise obtaining justice. It has been truly said that the inefficiency of the Government was largely to blame for the lawlessness of the Highlands. In those raids and vendettas there was much blood and cruelty. Life for such folk was a hard thing; they could suffer much, and were not chary of making others suffer; but even the brutality was governed by iron rules which were never infringed. There were laws not to be broken — the sanctitiy of an oath, the inviolability of a guest. Their life was like that of the Homeric heroes, cruel and brutish, but controlled by certain taboos which were absolute.

In actual comfort the society of the glen probably far exceeded that of a Lowland parish of the time. There was not the back-breaking monotonous toil on sour, ill-drained land. The chase gave their men healthy exercise. Their food was better, except in the depth of winter — full meals of flesh as contrasted with the Lowland sowens and bear-meal bannocks. Their bodies were better nourished and developed. If they had no Kirk to enforce discipline, they had a high-handed chief. Their houses were no worse, and fuel was more plentiful. Occupations were more varied, there was more social freedom, and more light and colour in their lives. They were worse citizens of Scotland, and of the world, than the peasants of Penpont or Muirkirk, but in their own enclave they had a richer and more wholesome civic life.

The keynote of such a society was a sense of ancient civilisation and a pride of race, in which every member of the clan shared. The long past of Clan Donald was an intimate thing to the humblest, almost like a living memory. They could not forget that the sons of Ian Abrach descended straight from that Angus Og of Islay who was also the father of the first Lord of the Isles. Tales ran in their heads of which their own kin had been the heroes, for there was no saga of the Isles in which they could not claim a part. And not Clan Donald alone, but their own little people had made a name for valour that rang through the Highlands. Ninety years back had not certain Moray lairds brought Alasdair Maclan Og of Glencoe to Morayland on a bond of maintenance to fight in their quarrels? A Glencoe man had guided Montrose in his famous descent upon Argyll.

The life in the glen, too, had its refinements and its hours of merriment. On the summer evenings on the haughs there would be tossing the cabar, and races among the young men, and fierce games of shinty. Up in the sheiling-huts in the twilight the girls would spin, or dance to the pipes, or listen to old tales and harpers' tunes. In the winter nights, when the birch billets made the peat fires leap, and the doors were shut, there would be snug gatherings; the old men at their tobacco, the wives at the spinning-wheel, and the young folk at their songs and tales. For great verse had been left to this little clan. Then would be heard the high deeds of Finn and Oscar, Caolte and Oisin, and the tragical tale of Deirdre, and a motley of adventures that made the breath catch and the blood run quick. Some of the stories came very near to them, for not twenty miles away to Loch Etive side had come the sons of Uisnach. Some of the songs, too, were their own. It was in the dark slit of Coire Gabhail that the fairies had whispered to the herd-girl the tune of *Crodh Chailean,* "Colin's Cattle", the most effective of

Life in the glen had its hours of merriment.

all milking songs, and the sweetest of lullabies.

By the 8th of January Maclan was back in Glencoe, somewhat weary, but with a mind at peace. He summoned at once Achtriachtan and the tacksman of Inverrigan.

"You have letters of protection from the Governor of Inverlochy," he said, "but they are not enough. You and all the males of my people must journey to Inveraray to take the oath, once the roads are open. Meantime I have sworn on your behalf, to see that Glencoe keeps the Government's peace. I have had kindness from Colin of Ardkinglas, and it must be repaid in strict honour. My children must bide as quiet in this glen as a hedgehog in its winter's hole. I, Maclan, have sworn it."

He asked for news, and was told that word had come by way of Mamore that Glengarry and his clan were up, and that some of Argyll's men, under Robert of Glenlyon, had gone out against them. He frowned at the name.

"Robert of Glenlyon is a bad person to be loose in Lochaber. Does son Alasdair know that his bonny kinsman is so near? It was an ill day for Appin when he took auld Glenlyon's widow to wife."

For the rest of January there were snow-storms which levelled the clefts with the braes; frosts, too, which made every waterfall a stack of silver spears. But that was on the high hills; in the valley bottom the fall soon melted. Now and then came soft mild days when the pastures showed bleached and sodden, and Loch Triachtan was blue with the reflection of the skies — the weather when, according to the Gaelic saying, the badger turns in his winter sleep and dreams of spring. The people of the glen, who had had anxious minds at the New Year, turned again to their several avocations. The women made the dyes of lichen and heather and seaweed for the wool they had spun, or wove that wool into plaiding; the old men mended cobles and steadings; and the young men were on the hill all day, bringing back fat hinds, and now and then a ptarmigan, or ranging the woods for roebuck and capercailzie, or on the shores of Loch Triachtan at sunset when the wild duck gathered.

Meantime, as we have seen, there was much afoot in London, and the posts to the north carried fateful letters. Livingstone, the commander-in-chief, received the King's instructions, dated January 16, and a covering letter from the Master of Stair. The Master on the same date wrote to Hill at Inverlochy, giving the details of the plan as arranged with Breadalbane — Argyll and Breadalbane watching the southern passes, the laird of Weem cutting off all retreat into Perthshire (with a special eye to the friendly Atholl clans), and a detachment from Hill's garrison blocking escape towards the Moor of Rannoch. Forbes, Hill's major, picked up this letter in Edinburgh, and, according to his instructions from his superior, broke the seals and forwarded it to Inverlochy. On his journey thither at the end of the month — he travelled by Lorn and Appin — he fell in with some of Argyll's regiment at the ferry of Ballachulish, and learned that they were bound for quarters in Glencoe.

When he reached Inverlochy he was in a sad state. He had received the King's instructions and the Master's letter, and disliked the whole business. After getting the message from Ardkinglas he had given orders that the Maclans should be considered loyal subjects and in no way molested, and now here was a plan in train to root them out, a very different treatment to that proposed for the still rebellious Glengarry. That was bad enough, bad, he thought, as public policy, besides being a rebuff to himself. But what perturbed him more was Forbes's account of what he had seen at Ballchulish. Soldiers of the Argyll regiment, but all Breadalbane's men, and seeking lodging in Glencoe! It looked as if some hideous piece of foul play were being meditated. He had virtually been superseded, too, for Livingstone was sending instructions direct to Hamilton, his second-in-command, and it was Hamilton who was managing the affair without confiding to him the details. His humanity and his professional dignity were alike outraged.

But what could he do? He could send in his papers. That would not stop the mischief, though it would ease his mind. The honest man was in a sad quandary. His conscience pricked him, but he remembered the monies due to him by the Crown, and the pension and knighthood which still tarried. He thought of his daughters and his lonely old age. So he decided to stand back, wash his hands of the whole concern, and do nothing except what his official duty demanded.

Livingstone was now writing direct to Hamilton, exhorting him on January 16th not to "trouble the Government with prisoners"; and on the 30th of the month we have seen that the Master wrote to Livingstone with an ominous postscript, and to Hill urging him to make the King's justice as conspicuous in the case of the Maclans as his clemency had been in other cases. But Hill was of no account now, and only Hamilton mattered. He it was who fixed the day for the attack, arranged the different parties, and selected the leaders. He seems to have been a competent soldier, ambitious to succeed in his profession, and apt to complain of slow promotion. We find both Livingstone and the Master telling him that his future depends upon how he makes use of the opportunities they offer him. The men he picked were mostly Breadalbane's own people, and, though no letters on the subject are extant, it is certain that the most heinous treachery in the business was devised by Breadalbane and ordered by Hamilton. Treachery, indeed, was, as we have seen, inherent in the plan if it was to be "secret and sudden," but the special form adopted was in such utter defiance of every Highland tradition that it could only have proceeded from the brain of one long destitute of honour, and have been executed by a time-serving Lowlander to whom Highlanders were no better than beasts of chase and warren. The actual operations, too, could only be entrusted to men who, body and soul, were Breadalbane's creatures.

The general scheme of netting Glencoe, though not its exact details, was known to the whole staff of the Inverlochy garrison. Hill did nothing. Two officers protested, and were put under arrest and sent prisoners to Glasgow. We do not know at what stage they made their protest, but it is possible that it was not till the actual day of the tragedy, when they were in Hamilton's company and saw the horrors with their own eyes. In that case their names were Francis Farquhar and Gilbert Kennedy.

The Jacobite journalist got an apt title for his pamphlet on Glencoe from the Emperor Gallienus, whose instructions to his ministers, after the defeat of Ingenuus in Illyricum, put Breadalbane's notions about extirpation in frank Latin. "Non mihi satisfacies, si tantum armatos occideris, quos et fors belli interimere potuisset. Perimendus est omnis sexus virilis, si et senes atque impuberes sine reprehensione nostra occidi possent. Occidendus est quicumque male voluit . . . Lacera, occide, concide."

On Monday the first day of February word came to Glencoe that a body of soldiers was approaching by the shore road from Ballachulish. The news spread like wild-fire, and every Maclan who had a sword or a musket hastened to bury it deep in the peat-stacks, or in a cairn of stones, or in some cunning place in the thatch. They had the Government's protection, but they did not wish to give up their arms, without which in those lawless times they felt themselves at the mercy of any ill-wishers. Moreover, the young men had their hunting to think of. John, the chief's eldest son, with twenty Maclans in his tail, waited at the foot of the glen to find out the errand of the strangers.

He saw a force of one hundred and twenty men in red coats and grey breeks, and a glance told him that they were of Argyll's regiment. At the head strode one whom he knew well. It was a tall man, with a long thin face, a hooked nose, a small petulant mouth like a girl's, and a delicate pointed chin. He wore his own hair, which was flaxen and scarcely tinged with grey, though his age was sixty. His complexion was still youthful, but his eyes had the glazed look of one much addicted to the bottle. The man carried himself well, and at the first glance seemed a model of manly beauty; it was only the second that showed the ravages of time and indulgence . . . There was no mistaking their kinsman of Glenlyon.

John, the chief's son, saw a force of 120 men in red coats.

Robert Campbell of Glenlyon had been born to a good but encumbered estate, and in his youth he had made ducks and drakes of it. He had been a notorious gambler, a heavy drinker, and something of a dandy. His political ventures, too, had been unlucky, for he had been a friend of the ill-fated Argyll who had suffered death seven years before. Bit by bit he had had to sell his patrimony, till he became little more than a hanger-on of Breadalbane. Now poverty had made him a soldier, and for two years he had had a captain's commission in Argyll's regiment. He was a man, John knew, who could have no good-will to Glencoe, for had he not lost heavily in the *creagh* which MacIan and Keppoch had driven from his few remaining lands after Killiecrankie — that exploit about which Breadalbane had been so bitter at the Achallader meeting? Yet oddly enough he was kin by marriage to his brother Alasdair. His mother had taken Stewart of Appin as her third husband, and Alasdair's wife was her grand-daughter, and therefore Glenlyon's niece.

The remembrance of this marriage tie was not much comfort to John, as he advanced to meet the newcomers. If the red soldiers were coming to the glen, there was no man in the world he would not have preferred as their captain.

But Glenlyon greeted him with demonstrative affection. He had always been famous for his hearty manners.

"Here's a burden come to your back, cousin," he cried. "It's no doing of mine, but a poor soldier must obey orders. We've been out to redd up things Invergarry way. . . . No, that affair is not finished, but the weather was unchancy and the Colonel has called a halt. Inverlochy is like a cried fair, and they are so throng there that there was no house-room for my lads. So what with that, and what with this matter of the cess and hearth-money — weary fall the Parliament that is aye laying new taxes on us poor Highlandmen! — nothing would content the Colonel but he must pack us off to Glencoe. We seek only bed and bite and sup for a week or two. I know it's a heavy affliction, but I'll see that it's made as light for you as possible. If you're to have sodgers quartered on you, it's better that a friend and a kinsman should have the doing of it."

He laid his hand on John's shoulder, a fine figure of a man, flushed with the sharp weather, almost as tall as old Maclan himself, a trim soldier, but a fellow-Highlander too, with his green Campbell plaid buckled about his middle. He spoke with an easy geniality, before which the other's constraint melted.

"You are welcome, Glenlyon," John said, "you and your lads. It's not much that Glencoe has to offer, but it's all yours for the taking."

"'Deed I never doubted it," was the answer. "And how is the good man, your father? And my nevoy Sandy?" He called up the two other officers, whom he introduced as Lieutenant Lindsay and Ensign Lindsay. "Helen's kin,", he explained.

"Man, this is a fair family gathering, though it's a month too late for Hogmanay."

The troops came to Carnoch with John and Glenlyon walking side by side at their head. Maclan received them with the dignity of an erstwhile opponent, but the courtesy of a chief and a gentleman. The men would be billeted up and down among the cottages, and as for the officers they were given their choice of the principal dwellings, Carnoch, Achnacon, Inverrigan and Achtriachtan. It seemed that Glenlyon had already made his choice.

"Inverrigan for me," he cried in his hearty way. "I'll not be putting you to trouble on my account, Maclan. I'll leave Achtriachtan and Achnacon, too, to the sole enjoyment of their firesides. Inverrigan is the place for us, where I'll be in the heart of my folk — and of your kind folk."

There was a great bustle all that day allotting billets to the men and moving baggage. Glenlyon and the Lindsays dined with the chief, and the first grew merry. There was new-killed venison on the table, and mutton-ham, and salt beef from the mart; fresh oat-cakes were baked on the girdle, and Maclan set out his foreign brandy. It seemed that the Argyll men had brought few stores with them except a supply of French claret and *aqua vitae.*

"This is better than Inverlochy," Glenlyon cried in his husky drunkard's voice. "Here's a fesat of fat things, and up yonder there was nothing but thin kale and a thrawn auld wife of a Governor."

When the strangers had gone to their quarters, Maclan talked with his sons.

"I like it ill," said Alasdair. "Glenlyon never came to Glencoe for Glencoe's good. He's a fine couthy fellow, but the word I have heard of him is that his heart is rotten as peat!"

"Maybe so," said the old man. "But he is our guest and must be treated well. You can sleep easy in your bed, Sandy, for now we are doubly secure. We have the Government's protection, and these men have eaten our salt."

CHAPTER FIVE
The Thirteenth
of February

The hundred and twenty soldiers of Argyll's were billeted among the cottages, three in one house and five in another, according to the size of the cottar's family. They were given the best entertainment the glen could offer; not very lavish since it was winter-time, but, what with kippered salmon and occasional deer-meat, better than the meagre rations of Inverlochy. Such hospitality meant that the hosts had to go very bare themselves. Glenlyon and the two Lindsays were with the tacksman at Inverrrigan, but they had few meals at home. Maclan was living not at Carnoch but at his farm a little way up the stream which descends from the Bhuidhe glen, and near by the two houses of his sons John and Alasdair; at Achnacon was Achtriachtan's brother, and Achtriachtan himself, to share in the hospitable duties, often slept there. There were frequent dinner-parties and card-parties for the strangers, and almost every day Glenlyon came to Alasdair's house to drink his morning draught, and to salute Alasdair's wife, his kinswoman.

The days passed pleasantly and the weather was kind for the time of year. Deep snow lay on the high tops and in the passes, for the December and January drifts had never melted, but in the valley itself the land was bare and dry. The Argyll men were mostly Highlanders and Campbells, but there were a few Lowlanders who hung together and talked their own talk, since their lack of Gaelic kept them from much intimacy with the folk of the glen. There were regular drills, when Sergeant Barber tried to smarten up the newer recruits, and in the afternoons there were often sports in the haugh, running and wrestling and that *camanachd* or shinty which was the game of all Gaeldom.

Of an evening, while the gentry were at the cards or a brew of toddy, the commonalty in the cotages had their own recreations. Stories and songs went round the fire, and among these well-mannered people there were adroit reticences. No word was said, no tale was told, by a Maclan which could wound the Campbell pride; they spoke and sang of the common traditions of the Gael, and of those wars of William and James, and of William and Louis, which could be freely mentioned, since with the rank-and-file politics did not go deep. Also there was piping, mostly on the *feadan* or chanter, but sometimes a *piobaireachd* on the full set by a piper who knew his trade. Here, too, the airs were tactfully chosen. There were no tribal rants to awaken memories of the ancient feud between Clan Donald and Clan Diarmaid, and the pieces played were the classics known to all Albain, *The Macrae's March* and *A Kiss of the King's Hand,* and *Desperate Battle,* and once in a while the heart-breaking *Lament of Macruimen.* Sometimes, too, a Maclan would bow to his guests and play a sprig out of Lorn or Argyll to remind them of home.

None of the soldiers, except the sergeant, had any notion of the purpose of their visit. They found themselves quartered in a kinder place than the Inverlochy barracks, and did not ask further questions. They were absorbed into the life of the glen as if they had been in their native clachans. The gentry, too, seemed at ease. The Lindsays were lumpish, sullen youths, but Glenlyon was a travelled man and a gentleman, a merry companion, and, when sober, very fastidious in his breeding. He would talk of politics with a shrug of his shoulders and a twinkle of his eye which precluded any danger of offence; he had wonderful tales of his own doings and much scandal about

The soldiers were absorbed into the life of the glen.

the great; his manner was hearty amd endearing, and if in his cups he was prone to bragging, it was done with humour and good-fellowship. There was no guile in that wandering drunken eye.

So thought all except Alasdair. Maclan himself was strong on Glenlyon's simplicity. "A rattling through-other fellow," he said, "whose worst foe is himself. He was never a match for yon fox of Breadalbane, so he finds himself at sixty Breadalbane's gillie. It's the queer old *bodach* he'll be in another ten years. But I tell you the man's mind is honester than sets with his tartan or his service."

John had agreed, but Alasdair still had his doubts. Glenlyon seemed to him to be nervous about something, to be waiting for something which he half feared and half hungered for. He had detected strange looks passing between him and the sullen Lindsays. Also his wife, Glenlyon's own kin, had a woman's forebodings. She would wake him in the night to question him. A cheerful soul, like all the Appin folk, she seemed now to have fallen into a strange depression of spirit.

So the life went on for eleven days, till Friday, the 12th of February. That day the weather changed. The wind shifted to the north-east, and whined through the gullies of Aonach Eagach. "There will be snow ere evening," said the old men; "in twenty-four hours the corries will be flat with the braes."

There was a change, too, in Glenlyon's demeanour. The anxiety which Alasdair had detected in him seemed to be sharpened. There was no drilling that forenoon in the haughs; instead he ordered a route-march and sent a half-company swinging past Carnoch along the road to Ballachulish. Alasdair had seen him in secret confabulation with Sergeant Barber; he had also observed the sergeant talking privately to some of the soldiers, and had noted how their faces after his talk grew troubled and a little scared.

In the afternoon there were sports as usual in the meadows by Carnoch. This time they were a dismal business, for the soldiers seemed to have lost their zest for games, and the air had suddenly grown piercing cold. When Alasdair went into his house at the darkening his wife had a curious tale for him. A child had brought it, a child who had been at the sports and had watched them from beside the great boulder which some glacier long ago had brought down from the hills. The story was that a soldier, an Argyll man, had slapped the boulder with his hand and addressed it in Gaelic. *"Grey stone of the glen"*, he had said, *"great is your right to be here. Yet if you but knew what will happen this night, you would be up and away."*

Alasdair tried to reassure her. "An Argyllman's nonsense," he said. "They are the lads for daft speeches. Nothing will happen this night except an on-ding of snow." But she refused to be comforted; she repeated the tale to others, and because of it there were many sleepless that night — to their own salvation.

In the evening Glenlyon recovered his composure. More, he was in wild spirits. He summoned John and Alasdair to Inverrigan to a card-party, and with the two Lindsays they played till supper-time. He had been bidden to dine next day by Maclan, he told them, and to bring his officers. Oddly enough he did not invite the brothers to sup with him, but dismissed them about seven o'clock. "I have gotten news, he said, "news which will mean some work for me before bedtime. I fear our pleasant little family gathering is near its end. There's fresh trouble up Glengarry's way, and any hour we may have to take the road." He was sober, but yet he had the same high laugh and uncertain eye as when he was drunk. Alasdair turned away from Inverrigan with a mind as heavy as the sky above him, from which were hurrying the first couriers of the snow.

The orders had gone out. That morning at Inverlochy, Hill, with a sad heart, had given Hamilton the formal instructions passed on to him from the Master and Livingstone:—

"You are with four hundred of my regiment, and the four hundred of my lord Argil's regiment under the command of Major Duncanson, to march straight to Glenco, and there put in due execution the orders you have received from the Commander-in-chief."

His one slender comfort was that he could saddle the responsibility on Livingstone, who had been in direct correspondence with Hamilton.

Hamilton the same day sent a special runner to Ballachulish, where Major Robert Duncanson was lying. Duncanson was Argyll's man, not Breadalbane's, but his troops were mostly the latter's, and included that Captain Drummond who had been in charge at Barcaldine when Maclan journeyed to Inveraray. He thus instructed Duncanson: —

"Pursuant to the Commander-in-Chief's and my Colonell's orders to me for putting in execution the service against the rebells of Glenco, wherein you, with the party of the Earle of Argile's regiment now under your command, are to be concerned. You are therefore to order your affairs so that you be at the severall posts assigned you by seven of the clock tomorrow morning, being Saturday, and fall in action with them, at which I will endeavour to be with the party from this place at the post appointed them. It will be necessary the avenues minded by Lieut Campbell on the south side be secured, that the old fox nor none of his cubs get away. The orders are that none be spared, nor the Government troubled with prisoners, which is all I have to say to you till then."

He added a postscript: —

"Please to order a guard to secure the ferry, and the boats there; and the boats must be all on this side the ferry, after your men are over."

Duncanson at Ballachulish completed the chain by his orders to Glenlyon, which had only four miles to travel: —

"You are hereby ordered to fall upon the rabelle, the Macdonalds of Glenco, and to putt all to the sword under seventy. You are to have a special care that the old fox and his sones doe not escape your hands. You are to secure all the avenues, that no man escape. This you are to putt in execution at five of the clock precisely. And by that time, or very shorty after it, I will strive to be at you with a stronger party. If I do not come to you at five, you are not to tarry for me but to fall on. This is by the King's special commands, for the good and safety of the countrie, that these miscreants be cutt off root and branch. See that this be put in execution, without fear or favour. Else you may expect to be dealt with as one not true to King nor countrie, nor a man fitt to carry a commission in the King 's service. Expecting you will not faill in the fullfilling hereof, as you love yourselfe."

Hamilton had fixed seven as the hour with Duncanson, but Duncanson, assuming with reason that Hamilton's part came later, had chosen five for Glenlyon's attack. The tone of his instructions to the latter suggests that he had some fear lest his sojourn among the Maclans might have blunted his zeal. It was an exact and comprehensive scheme of destruction. Against a little clan of two hundred, at the moment unarmed, and numbering only half a hundred fencible men, nine hundred and twenty regular soldiers were unleashed. Duncanson had only four miles to travel in the winter dawn to reach the foot of the glen; Hamilton, moving through the night from Inverlochy, would, by way of Kinlochleven and the Devil's Staircase, come down on the upper end. A detachment of Argyll's men at Island Stalker would block esacpe through Appin, the laird of Weem was watching the Perthshire roads, and Breadalbane waited in the Glenorchy passes.

Alasdair went to bed, but not to sleep. It was his turn to be wakeful, and at last his anxiety drove him to half-dress himself and look out of doors. The snow had for the moment stopped falling, but there was promise of more in the wind, and it was bitter cold. Close to his house was an empty cottage used as a guard-room by the soldiers, and to his surprise he saw a light in it. It was just after midnight, when all should have been long in their beds. Then he heard footsteps in the snow, and several men entered the guard-room, including one who had the shape and carriage of the elder Lindsay. Much alarmed, he slipped off to his brother John's house, and woke him. John took the thing lightly and refused to move. "They are doubling the guards," he said, "and a very proper course. In this devil's weather the sentries need to be relieved often. That's the reason of the extra folk in the guard-room. Glenlyon's a careful man. Back to your bed, Sandy." Alasdair, half-frozen, returned to his own house, and presently was asleep.

By five o'clock on the morning of Saturday 13th the wind had grown to a tempest, and the snow was drifting heavily. About that hour Lieutenant Lindsay and a few soldiers presented themselves at Maclan's house, and asked civilly to see the chief on a pressing matter. They were at once admitted, and Maclan got out of bed and struggled into his trews, shouting to bring the visitors a morning draught. Suddenly two shots were fired at him from behind, one in the body and one in the brain, and the old man fell dead. Then mania seized on the murderers. Lady Glencoe — to give her the title which lairds' wives bore — had risen and dressed; they seized her, stripped her naked, and tore the rings from her fingers with their teeth. The sound of the firing had brought some of the near-by dwellers to the house. Two were shot dead, and one, Duncan Don, who had come with letters from the Braes of Mar, was badly wounded. Lindsay and his party flung the three corpses out of doors into the snow, and the wounded man, whom they took for dead, and then turned to leave. . . . Through the drift came another party to meet them, buffeting their way up from Loch Leven. It was Duncanson and his four hundred.

The gale blanketed the sound of the shots, and the chief's sons, whose houses were a little way off, heard nothing. But it was now John who was wakeful. Before the shooting began he heard the movement of troops outside his window; there was shouting, perhaps because some of the better disposed wished to give him the alarm. He rose, dressed, and ran to Inverrigan to find out what was happening from Glenlyon

Mania seized the murderers.

himself, apparently not dreaming of any danger to his father. He found Glenlyon up and dressed, and got a cheerful greeting. "What's the steer?" he cried. "The steer is that we're off to take order with Glengarry. What ails youi, man? You're as white as the snow on your plaid." Then he burst into his jolly laugh. "Feared for Glencoe? Is it likely? Is it likely I would lift my hand against my good friends, or if I was so ill-minded that I would not first pass the word to my nevoy Sandy? Back to your bed and thank God you have not to take the road in this hell-begotted weather."

John went home, only half-reassured, and lay down but did not undress. He may have dozed for an hour, not more. A servant rushed in and told him that, in a pause of the snow, he had seen soldiers moving towards his door. John went out and saw not fifty yards off a party of twenty redcoats, with their bayonets screwed into their musket-barrels. He had never seen them before, for they were Duncanson's men. . . . He knew the truth at last, and fled to the snow-laden scrub below the screes of Meall Mor.

There he stumbled upon another fugitive. Alasdair ten minutes earlier had been waked by his servant, who asked him if it were a time to sleep when they were killing his brother, for he had seen the soldiers with bayonets fixed approaching John's house. That which he had long dreaded had come to pass, and Alasdair acted on a plan already formed in his head. He got his little household through the snow to a place of temporary concealment, while he himself took to the hillside. Like John he did not think of his father's house, but of Inverrigan and Achnacon as the danger-points. So he ran along the slopes of the south wall of the glen in order to reconnoitre, and as he ran he met his brother. They stood and listened, for in the hollow below was the sound of guns — many guns. They came from Achnacon.

The murdering foxes butchered the clansfolk.

Sergeant Barber was busy there. Something had happened to alarm the household, for Achnacon himself was up and dressed, and was sitting by the fire with Achtriachtan his brother, and eight other men who had come in from the cottages. Suddenly there was a volley, and Achtriachtan fell dead, and four more. The others dropped on the floor, all wounded. Barber bent over Achnacon and asked him if he were alive. "I live," was the answer, "and I have but the one wish — if I must die, to die out of doors." "I have eaten your bread," said the sergeant, "so I will do you that kindness." He was led outside, and put up before the muzzles of the guns. But Achnacon was a powerful man, and wrath and fear made him desperate. He flung his plaid over the soldiers' faces, broke through the cordon, and made for the hills, while the other four inside managed to creep out by the back of the house. Barber made short work of those left in Achnacon hamlet. One was a child who was never seen again; only his hand was found; he may have died in the snow and been devoured by fox or eagle. The bodies of the dead were flung on to the midden and covered with dung.

At Inverrigan was Glenlyon. John had not long left him before the work of murder began. Nine men were taken, bound hand and foot, and shot. Then he seems to have sickened of the business and inclined to hold his hand. But Captain Drummond arrived from Duncanson's party, and as Breadal·bane's henchman he remembered his chief's orders. He and Barber seem to have been the most bloody-minded of the crew. Glenlyon had spared a lad of twenty. Drummond, who had the same military rank, reminded him of his instructions, and shot the youth dead. A boy of thirteen years ran out and clung to Glenlyon's knees; Glenlyon would have saved him, but he was pistolled by Drummond. A child of four or five years was among the victims, and a woman — an excess which even Gallienus had not commanded. The bodies were hastily shovelled into shallow graves.

It was the same in all the cottages. Wherever there was a living male who could be laid hands on he died by shot or steel. Among the victims was an old man of eighty. Then, when there was no life left, the soldiers turned to other work. They loosed the cattle from the byres, the sheep from the pens, and the shelties from the rude stables. As John and Alasdair strained their ears from the skirts of Meall Mor they heard the lowing of hungry animals, who had missed their morning meal of bog-hay. And as the February dawn turned the dark into grey, they saw the driving snow redden with a glare from the valley, and knew the cause. Every cottage and hut and hovel was going up in flames.

By eight o'clock the business was over, but Glenlyon and Duncanson had not fulfilled their masters' commands. To be sure, the Government was not going to be troubled with prisoners, but they had made but a poor killing. Thirty bodies at the most, and of them several were children and at least one a woman. Most of the younger men had escaped, and though the old fox was dead his cubs were still at large. They consoled themselves by reflecting that there was but one way out of Glencoe, and that Hamilton with his Inverlochy men was stopping that bolt-hole. So they turned to their task of burning and plundering with an easy mind.

But all was not well with Hamilton. He had marched by night down the shore road from Inverlochy, and long before dawn had reached Kinlochleven. There he split up his command into parties, each with its special instructions, but all with orders to slay every man they met and make no prisoners. But on their way across the hills by the Devil's Staircase they encountered so fierce a blizzard that they were obliged to repeatedly stop and take shelter. John Forbes, Hill's major, who unwillingly accompanied them, must have thanked heaven for the weather. What with one thing and another it was eleven in the forenoon before they found themselves at the upper end of Glencoe.

There they were met by Duncanson, who, weary of waiting, was making a patrol of the glen. He reported that old Maclan was dead and thirty-odd of his men, but that the rest had flown to the hills. Hamilton went down the river, killed an old man, burned one or two more houses, and realised that he could do nothing further. Through no fault of his own he had failed to carry out to the full the mission which was to bring him fame and fortune. His comfort was that the refugees in the hills were doomed, though they did not fall by his guns, for no human beings could live long in such a tempest of wind and ice. He contented himself with seeing to the booty, most of which would be the perquisite of the officers. The pitiful little belongings of the clan, clothes, trinkets, spoons and cups and platters, were already in the soldiers' pouches. Fatigue parties were appointed, and by the afternoon the whole stock of the glen, nine hundred cattle, two hundred horses, and a multitude of sheep and goats, were being driven across the narrows of Loch Leven on their way to Inverlochy.

Meantime what of the survivors of the little clan? The snow was their salvation, for in five yards a man was lost to sight in the drift, and they had the advantage of knowing the ground like their own steadings. Except for a young man there were but two winter roads out of Glencoe — one by the shore to Appin, and one by the east to Rannoch and Glenorchy. The first they knew was blocked by Duncanson, but they did not know of Hamilton's purpose to net the upper end. There was a third, which an active man might manage, the pass of the Laroch between Meall Mor and Ben Vair, but there, too, Duncanson was the barrier. The only hope was to go up the glen.

One or two hunters escaped by the mountain gullies, north into Mamore, and to the Macdonald dwellings on Loch Treig. But these routes were only for the mountaineer, and many desperate miles had to be covered before a place of safety was reached. In such weather it was necessary not only to get out of the clutches of the assassins but to find food and shelter, for even the hardiest could scarcely survive a night among the blizzards and snow-wreaths of the high corries.

There was only one ultimate sanctuary — Appin — for Keppoch was too distant. In Appin there would be refuge with a friendly people, a people strong enough, too, to defend the refugees. But how to get to Appin since the coast road was shut. There were two possible routes — one by the Bhuidhe glen: a second through the Lairig Gartain, between the Shepherds of Etive to Dalness; after that the way lay down Glen Etive, where there were only shepherds' bothies, to the head of the sea-loch, and then across the low *beallach* to Glen Ure and Glen Creran. Local tradition declares that most of the people escaped by the first road, but it is certain that in winter weather it was possible only for the young and the strong. The weaker folk must have followed the second. Before it was yet light, while Glenlyon and Duncanson were burning the clachans and driving out the cattle, men, women and children, old and young, many of them half-naked, were struggling up the glen in the teeth of the storm. Once they were past Loch Triachtan they were out of the danger of the troops. The Devil's Staircase descends the northern wall opposite the opening of the Lairig Gartain, but the fugitives were inside the pass long before Hamilton appeared from Mamore.

It was a cruel journey, for the snow still drifted. There were grandfathers and grandmothers among them, women heavy with child, mothers with infants at the breast, sick folk and the very young. To their bewilderment and terror were soon added the pangs of hunger, fatigue and an extreme cold. Such as reached Dalness found temporary shelter and entertainment, for the tenant was a Maclan whom Breadalbane's men had strangely omitted to molest. But some died on the road thither, and more on the further road down the Etive or over the *beallach* to Glen Ure. Among the latter was Lady Glencoe, her fingers torn by the teeth of Lindsay's troops. Some thirty were murdered in the glen, and as many perished from the hardships of the flight. But in the end Appin was reached, and there the Maclans found roofs to cover them, and a share of Appin's scanty winter provender, and armed Stewarts to protect them should their enemies follow. In Appin the little clan was nursed back to life.

By the afternoon of the 13th Glencoe was a silent place. Scorched thatch still smoked among the snow-drifts, and ravens barked above the blood-smears on the blackened thresholds. From Aonach Eagach and Aonach Dubh the eagles and buzzards were gathering where the corpses had been left unburied. Except for these there was no sound — save that from Loch Leven shore came the far-away echo of Glenlyon's pipes. The tune they played was *The Glen is Mine.*

CHAPTER SIX
The Reckoning

Glencoe was left to the peace of death, and soon the snow shrouded the charred roof-trees and the bloody hearthstones. Hamilton, Duncanson and Glenlyon reported at Inverlochy. Their plan had somewhat miscarried, but the Maclans were fugitives in the winter hills, and it was predicted that the weather would complete the half-done job. That the affair had been bungled could not be denied. The alarm had been given by using muskets instead of cold steel, and Hamilton had signally failed to stop the main exit. Both Hill and Hamilton made their reports to the Master of Stair, who could only express a very moderate satisfaction. "All I regret is that any of the sept got away, and there is necessity to prosecute them to the utmost. If they could go out of the country, I could wish they were let slip, but they can never do good there. Appin, who is the heritor, should have encouragement to plant the place with other people than Macdonalds." By way of a reward to Hill he promised to look into his money claims against the Government, and to take up the matter of the civil jurisdiction for which he had long been pressing.

But strange rumours were beginning to spread, coming from the talk, perhaps, of the more merciful among the soldiers, or by devious ways from the fugitives. By March 5 there was a story in London that the Maclans had been murdered in their beds after taking the oath; the Master of Stair denied the latter part of the report, but not the first. In Edinburgh the rumour was more detailed. Argyll's regiment had been ordered south, and Glenlyon was in Edinburgh on his way to England. He was drinking heavily, and boasting at large in the coffee-houses. People noticed the wildness of his manner and the uncertainty of his eye, which belied his bold words. Bit by bit from his babbling the story came out. He was robustly impenitent. He declared that he and his colleagues were supplicating the Council for some special recognition of their meritorious services. "I would do it again," he cried. "I would stab any man in Scotland or England, if my master the King ordered me, and never speir the cause. He who would not do that is no loyal subject." But he was like a "fey" man, with a catch in the voice and sudden terrors in the face.

In April Glencoe was the chief talk of the Scottish capital. On April 12 the Paris *Gazette* published a summary of the doings there, accurate except in so far as it said that Maclan's two sons had perished with him. The Jacobites had been miraculously given new powder and shot, and they were not slow in using it. In April a pamphlet appeared in London, in the form of a letter from Scotland, which told correctly the full tale. At first its horrors were not realised, for the Jacobite journalists were fond of making people's flesh creep, and did not enjoy any very high repute for veracity. But bit by bit came confirmatory evidence, damning proofs that could not be denied, and by the summer responsible people in Edinburgh and London knew

beyond question a horrid barbarity had been committed.
Argyll's regiment was now quartered at Brentford on its way to
Flanders, and its private soldiers were talking. Charles Leslie,
the Jacobite, went out on June 30 to see them and got the full
details. Both Glenlyon and Drummond were there, and, said
one of the men, "Glencoe hangs about Glenlyon night and day,
and you may see him in his face." But William had gone to his
glorious and inconclusive wars, and the fall of Namur and the
preparations for Steenkirk left him no time for the trivialities of
Lochaber.

    Secretly during the spring the Maclans began to creep
back to Glencoe. First went the young men to bury the dead
and report that there was nothing stirring in the glen. Then a

few of the half-burned cottages were made habitable, and when the fine weather began some cattle were brought to the haughs, the gift of kindly neighbours. John and Alasdair, who knew that Hill was not ill-disposed to them, approached him for help, and accordingly on May 3 the Scottish Privy Council authorised him to grant personal protection — "to these persons, either in general or particularly, of all security to their persons, lands and goods, and a cessation of all acts of hostility, trouble or molestation to them, upon the account of their having been in arms and rebellion against their Majesties, and to take what security he shall think meet for their living peaceably until his Majesty signifies his pleasure therein."

Secretly during the Spring the Maclans began to creep back to Glencoe.

It was not much of a grace, for the Maclans had no goods
to protect, but it enabled them to set to work to rebuild their
shattered life. On October 3, Hill, having got the royal assent,
formally received Glencoe into the King's peace, Alasdair
acting on behalf of the clan. Four days later he wrote to the laird
of Culloden: "The Glencoe men are abundantly civil. I have put
them under my lord Argyle, and have Arkenloss' surety for
them till my lord comes; for they are now my Lord Argyle's
men; for't was very necessary they should be under some
person of power, and of honesty to the Government."
Ardkinglas throughout the whole miserable buisness showed
himself consistently honourable and humane.

But this formal pacification, and the paradox of a
Campbell becoming surety for a Macdonald, did not silence the
rumours. It was in the interest of the Jacobites to foster them,
and even the tough conscience of seventeenth-century
Scotland was disquieted. In April 1693, Livingstone wrote to
Hamilton that "some in Parliament make a talking about the
business of Glencoe, and give out that they design to have it
examined," and a month later he grew seriously concerned,
and told the same correspondent that Hill must come to
Edinburgh to tell all he knew. "It is not that anybody thinks that
thieving tribe did not deserve to be destroyed, but that it should
have been done by such as were quartered amongst them,
makes a great noise. I suppose I may have pressed it somewhat
upon your Colonel, knowing how slow he was in the execution
of such things."

It was a great noise indeed, for every opponent of the
Government was soon in full cry, not from love of Glencoe, but
from hatred of Stair. Some honest souls had indeed been
horrified by the tale, and for humanity's sake would fain have
punished the guilty. When the Master of Stair resigned the
office of Lord Advocate, Sir John Lauder of Fountainhill
refused to accept it unless he was permitted to prosecute the
Glencoe murderers. But the main motive was politics, not

justice. The Master was too powerful not to have numberless enemies, and too passionately wise to have many friends among the *politiques;* Johnston of Wariston, his colleague, was intriguing against him; while, of the extremists, the Jacobites hated him as a traitor and the enthusiasts as the enemy of true religion.

In 1693 William, induced by his tender-hearted Queen, ordered the Lord High Commissioner, the Duke of Hamilton, to institute an inquiry into the methods used in Glencoe, of which the tales grew daily wilder. But Hamilton died, and nothing was done in that Parliament. The scuffling of kites and crows in Lochaber seemed to the King of small importance compared to the thorny ecclesiastical questions which were obtruding themselves in Parliament and General Assembly. But when the House met again in the early summer of 1695 it was clear that an inquiry would be insisted upon. William anticipated the demand, and, before leaving for the Continent, he appointed a commission, under the presidency of Tweeddale, the new High Commissioner. After three weeks Parliament began to clamour for the report, and, though technically it should have been first submitted to William in Flanders, the agitation was so great that Tweeddale was compelled to produce it on June 24.

The commission did its work with expedition and thoroughness. It took the evidence of the chief surviving Maclans, and of other Highlanders, and it had before it the letters which had passed between the Master of Stair, Livingstone, Hill, and Hamilton. Its decisions may be briefly summarised. A great wrong had been done in not presenting Maclan's certificate of submission to the Scottish Privy Council; not a very relevant point, considering that his submission was known in London, and one probably introduced to make prejudice against the elder Stair. The Master knew about Maclan's oath, and, though aware that the King had admitted Glengarry, who was in worse case, into mercy, did not countermand the general order for a massacre. The Master's letters showed that he had interpreted "extirpation" in a different sense to the King, and had thereby exceeded his instructions and caused "a barbarous murder."

Parliament proceeded to debate the matter in detail. Hill was called before them and exonerated. A warrant was granted for the citation of Hamilton, who fled the country. The King was asked to send home for trial Major Duncanson, Captain Drummond, Lieutenant Lindsay and Sergeant Barber, who were serving in Flanders and so beyond the reach of the ordinary law. On July 10 the House in an address to the King extolled his mercy, for reasons which are not apparent, demanded the prosecution of the minor offenders from Hamilton downwards, and decided that Hill and Livingstone were covered by the orders of the Secretary of State. Then it turned to the Master, the true quarry that the hounds had always in view. "We beg your Majesty will give such orders about him, for vindication of your Government, as you in your Royal wisdom shall think fit."

The inquiry had been honest, but not so the findings of the commission or the resolution of Parliament. It is difficult to resist Macaulay's argument that the subordinates were covered by their military duty, and, whatever their moral guilt, were legally blameless. If this plea be disallowed, then why did not the blame attach throughout the whole hierarchy, up through Hill and Livingstone to the King? If it be argued that the worst horror, "murder under trust," which especially shocked the public mind, was due to Hamilton's specific orders, it may be answered that some kind of treachery was implicit in all the orders both of Livingstone and the Master, since they insisted on quiet and secrecy, though they did not contemplate the hideous sadism of the actual deeds. It was a mere quibble which exonerated William while it condemned the Master, and a worse quibble which concentrated on the minor malefactors and did not ask for the Master's trial. Policy over-rode justice, for

Parliament knew that the King would never surrender Stair, and moreover that, if he was brought to trial, that trial would be a farce without the King as a witness. No doubt it was also aware that Breadalbane stood behind the whole business, but had been too wary to leave one scrap of incriminating evidence. He was indeed arrested and sent to Edinburgh Castle for the treasonable secret clauses arranged at Achallader in June 1691, but his defence was accepted that he only arranged these clauses to get to the bottom of the Jacobite plots, and he was presently released.

William did nothing. In common decency he could do nothing, for he knew that a great part of the moral responsibility was his own. He removed the Master from the Scottish Secretaryship — he could hardly do less in view of the finding of Parliament; and the Scottish politicians, having got their way, turned joyfully to the Darien adventure. But he gave him an indemnity, "his Majesty being willing to pardon, forgive and remit any excess of zeal in going beyond his instructions by the said John Viscount Stair, and that he had no hand in the barbarous manner of execution"; and as a token of his favour granted him the teinds of the regality of Glenluce in his own Galloway country.

The Jacobite hope *Qui Glencoat Glencoabitur* was never realised. Hamilton was indeed put to the horn and disappears from history, but no punishment fell on the three Lowlanders who were guilty of the worst barbarities — Drummond, Lindsay and Barber. Hill got his knighthood — and, let us hope, his pension, for he was an honest if ineffectual being — but he did not live long to enjoy it. Livingstone became Viscount Teviot. Glenlyon had risen to be a colonel before he died at Bruges in August 1696. As for Breadalbane, he continued his infamies to an extereme old age. He was deep in the Jacobite attempt of 1707, and, when he was nearly eighty, he rose with Mar in the

'Fifteen, and managed to shuffle out after Sheriffmuir. He advised Mar's officers, since they were good for nothing else, to buy a printing press and start a newspaper! The old reprobate had not one rag of virtue, but he had a sense of humour.

Of the two greater figures in the tragedy, the Master of Stair was occluded for a brief time from the service of the State. He ventured a thousand pounds in the Darien scheme, which he doubtless lost. In 1695 he succeeded his father as second viscount; in 1702 he was a privy councillor, and in 1703 Anne made him an earl. He was the ablest Scotsman of his day — the man, said Defoe, "of greatest counsel in the kingdom." He was among the chief architects of the Union, but died of apoplexy at the age of fifty-nine, on the eve of its final ratification. Unloved and unloving, careless of common esteem, he found such happiness as was permitted him in the exercise of his superb intelligence and in a cynical condescension to the follies of mankind.

As for the King, he marched resolutely upon his appointed way, through success and unsuccess, bereavement and broken health, till that February day in 1702 when the molehill of the "little gentleman in black velvet," long to be toasted by the Jacobites, brought down his horse at Hampton Court, and he died a few months after the exiled James. William was a great man and a great European statesman, but to Scotland he meant little. He had to bear much of the blame for two dismal tragedies, Glencoe and Darien. The Edinburgh mob forced the bell-ringers of St Giles's to play the tune of "Wilful Willie." Seasons of bitter famine, for which he got the credit, coincided with his continental wars. On the 8th of March 1702, the day of his death, a Highland widow announced to her neighbours the good tidings. When asked how she knew, her answer was that her cow had given twice as much milk as she had had from her for seven years.

The Parliament of Scotland recommended that the survivors of Glencoe might have some reparations made to them for their losses and be supplied with the necessaries of life. Nothing was done, except that the Privy Council instructed the authorities of Argyll not to press for payment of the cess. Yet the little clan managed to creep back to a certain stability. John, as chief, drew the survivors together, and, aided by Appin and Keppoch and Glengarry, built up their shattered life. He died after building a new house at Carnoch, and his successor was the child of two who had been carried to the hills by his nurse on the morning of the massacre. The clan would appear to have grown in numbers. In 1745 Duncan Forbes, the Lord President, put the fighting men at one hunded and fifty, and the report of the minister of Inverness a year later rated them at one hundred. Better seasons and the growing wealth of the Lowlands had no doubt improved the trade in black cattle and skins and increased their means of livelihood.

There was to be one final drama in the story of the glen before the broken lights of its past faded into common day. The chief, Alasdair, and his twin brothers, James and Donald, rose in the 'Forty-five. They joined Prince Charles Edward on August 27 with one hundred and twenty men; Alasdair was a member of the Prince's Council and fought in all his battles. After Culloden he was attainted, and lay some years in prison, but he was alive in the glen in 1773. The high moment of the Maclans was in the march to Edinburgh, when the Prince's army occupied Linlithgow. Nearby stood the house of Newliston, a Stair dwelling which the Master had got in virtue of his wife. Alasdair demanded that his men and no others should guard Newliston, that they might prove to the world that the purity of the cause for which they fought was smirched by no "vileinye of hate."

The last word — and a great word — was with Glencoe.

Scottish bestsellers from **Lang**Syne

Story of a Nation

From the dawn of time to the 21st century discover your land and the land of your forefathers.

If you think the pageant of Scottish history is only a catalogue of murder and mayhem, of fratricide and civil war, this book will make you think again. Most of Scotland's problems did not arise because the Scots were a greedy and expansionist nation, but because we were all too frequently involved in fending off powerful neighbours who coveted our soil.

For many decades Professor Hume Brown's work has stood the test as an accurate record, telling our nation's story in a bright, concise style. In 1961 Dr. H. W. Meikle, the Historiographer-Royal for Scotland, fully edited the text and wrote fresh chapters in light of new developments and discoveries.

In 1990 Rennie McOwan, the distinguished writer, updated the text yet again and further revisions have been made to the subsequent editions.

Today, after a referendum in September 2014, where the vote for independence was 45 per cent for and 55 per cent against, Scotland is at a new crossroads.

As further key powers are devolved to the Scottish Parliament in Edinburgh our nation's epic journey continues to hold a compelling fascination.

ISBN 978-1-85217-170-4   £12.99

Scottish Proverbs

A wise and often hilarious compilation of Scottish wit and wisdom garnered over the centuries.

Countless topics are covered in a comprehensive A - Z format, with many witty illustrations.

Read how to chart your course through life with the aid of some choice Caledonian couthiness, like "it's a sair time when a mouse looks oot o' the meal barrel wi' a tear in its eye" or "a man may dig his grave wi' his teeth" and many, many more.

ISBN 978-0-94626-408-7   £5.99

Bonnie Prince Charlie and Flora MacDonald

Bonnie Prince Charlie's campaign to become King of Great Britain ended in disaster on the bloody battlefield of Culloden Moor. And for months afterwards he was a fugitive, hunted by Government troops across the Highlands and Islands of Scotland.

Although a huge reward, worth £1 million in today's terms, was offered for information that would lead to his arrest not a single Highlander betrayed the brave and gallant Charles Edward Stuart.

Indeed many risked their lives and those of their families by helping him to escape. And of this brave and gallant band the most daring was a young woman called Flora MacDonald. It was Flora, then just 24, who disguised the Prince as her Irish spinning maid, Betty Burke, and smuggled him out of Scotland under the noses of thousands of English redcoats.

In this double volume George Forbes charts the course of the rebellion from the moment Prince Charles landed at Eriskay on August 3, 1745, while Alexander MacGregor focuses on the remarkable life of Flora MacDonald, the heroine who was prepared to lay down her life for her Prince.

ISBN 978-1-85217-008-0   £5.99

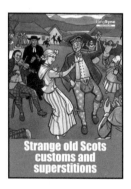

Strange old Scots customs and superstitions

The Scots have always been superstitious.

Our ancestors were savages who painted their faces, believed in magic and worshipped the sun, offering human sacrifices to their gods.

Some ancient customs have survived to the present day while others, thankfully, have passed into history.

ISBN 978-0-94626-405-6   £5.99

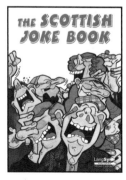

The Scottish Joke Book

Here's a great selection of jokes and stories that will have you laughing all the way from Dumfries to Durness. You'll have a smile as wide as the Clyde as we serve up a fantastic fund of gags you'll be able to retell friends and family.

Our publisher is certainly smiling. This is his biggest seller since the previous chart-topper, *Exit Signs – are they on the way out?*

ISBN 978-1-85217-105-6   £3.99

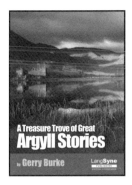

A Treasure Trove of Great Argyll Stories

How Government officers framed a man for murder to stop another Jacobite Rebellion.

The church with a phantom handprint, a piper executed for playing the wrong tune and the secret silver coin of doom. The remarkable story of Oban – its boom times and the saga of the unfinished colosseum.

How Inveraray achieved global fame, the grim secrets of the castles around Loch Awe and the soldiers who chose a hangman's rope rather than a life as street beggars.

These pages deliver what the title promises – a treasure trove of great Argyll stories. Read about the king who had the heads of clansmen cut off and half boiled. Discover the ancient civilisations who had their homes in Argyll at the dawn of history and find out what happened when Viking invaders declared it their "island" home. Read about the hydro power pioneers who died in dire straits, the secrets of the travelling folk, mayhem wrought by gangsters of the sea, a grave cursed for eternity, a modern Robinson Crusoe and much, much more.

ISBN 978-1-85217-176-6   £5.99

Folk Tales of the Highlands

The Highlands and Islands of Scotland are rich in strange stories and folk tales. Read about the seven brothers who were slaughtered by the Giant of Jura, the drowned sailors who came back to life as seals, buried treasure and the vanity of two giants which turned a life of poverty into a life of prosperity for folk living in a glen beside Loch Shiel.

Faeries, brownies, water-horses, ghosts, witches, wells said to cure all kinds of disease, adventures from the Jacobite Rebellions – this book has something for everyone.

ISBN 978-1-85217-011-0   £5.99

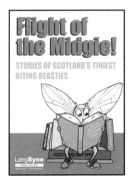

Flight of the Midgie!

Stories of Scotland's tiniest biting beasties.

Here it is, all you ever wanted to know – and a bit more besides – about the scourge of Scotland...the dreaded MIDGIE!

Read about its history, folklore and news stories. Appreciate the poems it inspired, the hilarious short stories it stung with inspiration. Discover the zoological facts and little known traits of the wee beastie. Above all, learn how to combat once and for all this scunner of the glens!

ISBN 978-1-85217-116-2   £4.99

Whisky

Here is the quintessential guide to everything you wanted to know about Scotch whisky.

Inside you will find all the relevant facts to do with your favourite classic malts, how 'the water of life' had its origins in mystic medieval times in ancient Caledonia, how bold smugglers risked life and limb to escape the dreaded customs men, the real story behind the fortuitous shipwreck of Whisky Galore!, a tour of the top distilleries and much, much more…

So sit down, relax and savour this appreciation of the world's favourite tipple.

Cheers!

ISBN 978-1-85217-568-9
£5.95

GATHERING OF THE CLANS

CLAN MEMORABILIA FROM LANG SYNE

Books, Postcards, Teddy Bears, Keyrings, Coasters, Magnets and much more...

Visit our website:

www.langsyneshop.co.uk

or write to us:
Lang Syne Publishing,
79 Main Street, Newtongrange, Midlothian EH22 4NA
Tel: 0131 344 0414   Fax: 0845 075 6085
E-mail: info@lang-syne.co.uk